Power Maths

Year 1 Tex... A

Series Editor: Tony Stan...

Flo

Flo is flexible and creative.

She likes to find new ways to solve problems.

brave

Astrid

curious

Ash

determined

Dexter

helpful

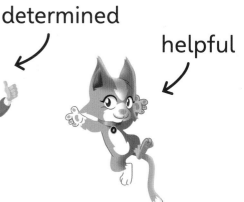

Sparks

Pearson

Contents

This shows us what page to turn to.

Let's start our maths journey!

3

How to use this book

Let's see how Power Maths works!

These pages help us get ready for a new unit.

Discover

Lessons start with Discover.

Have fun exploring new maths problems.

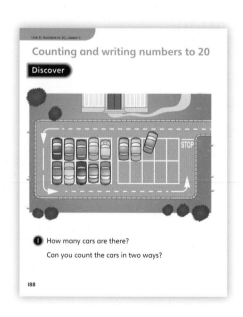

Share

Next, we share what we found out.

Did we all solve the problems the same way?

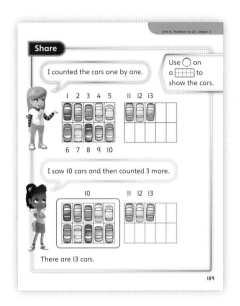

Think together

Then we have a go at some more problems together.

We will try a challenge too!

This tells you which page to go to in your Practice Book.

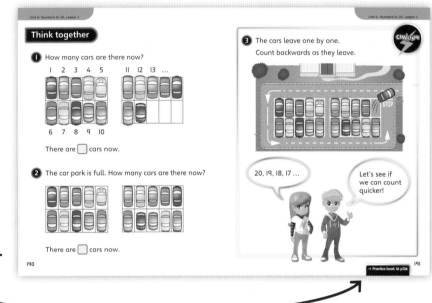

At the end of a unit we will show how much we can do!

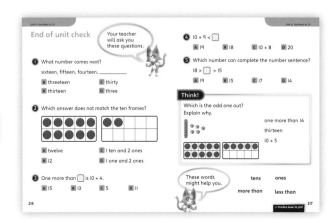

Unit 1
Numbers to 10

In this unit we will …
- ⚡ Sort and count objects to 10
- ⚡ Count and write to 10
- ⚡ Count backwards from 10 to 0
- ⚡ Count one more and one less
- ⚡ Compare and order numbers
- ⚡ Learn to use a number line

You can count to find how many there are. How many  are there?

1	2	3	4	5
⚡	⚡	⚡	⚡	⚡

We will need some maths words. Do you know some of these?

Sort   Groups   Digits   Count back

One more   One less   Matched

Fewer   Greater than   Equal to

Most   Least   Fewest

Greatest   Number line

Do you remember how to say these numbers? Count to 10!

1 2 3 4 5 6 7 8 9 10

Sorting objects

Discover

1 **a)** Sort the ⃝ and ⬡ into two **groups**.

b) Sort the fruit. What groups did you make?

Share

a)

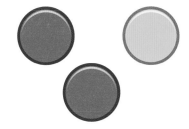

There is a group of counters and a group of cubes.

    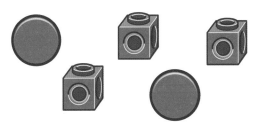

These are red.   These are yellow.

b)

I wonder if I can sort the fruit into 2 groups?

A group of apples, a group of oranges, a group of bananas.

A group of round fruit and a group of non-round fruit.

9

Think together

1 Sort into groups. Circle the other group with your finger.

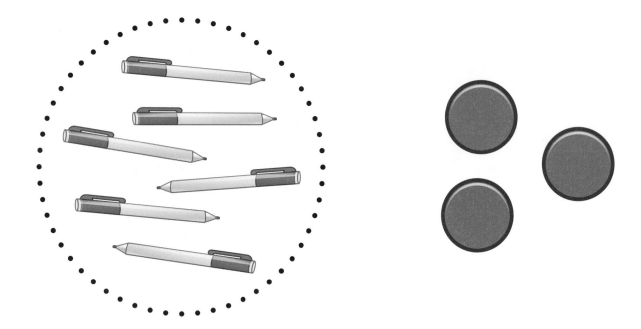

2 Sort into groups. Circle the groups with your finger.

3 Sort in two different ways.

Is there another way?

→ Practice book 1A p6

Counting objects to 10

Discover

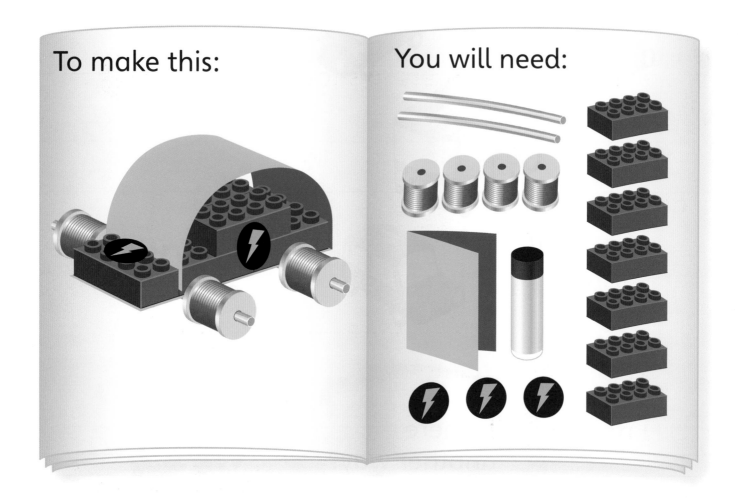

To make this:

You will need:

1 **a)** How many ⚡ do you need?

b) How many 🧱 do you need?

Share

I will count them. I, 2, 3 …

I can use counters to show how many  .

a)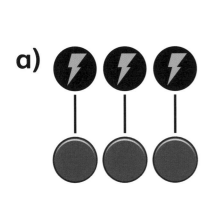

There are 3 counters.

I need 3 .

b)

I need 7 🧱 .

Think together

1 How many  do you need?

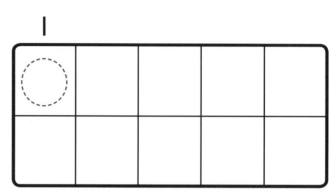

There is ☐ counter.

I need ☐  .

2 How many  do you need?

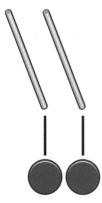 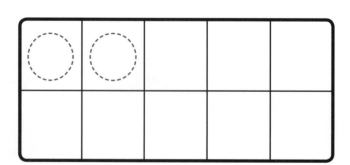

There are ☐ counters.

I need ☐  .

CHALLENGE

3 **a)** How many 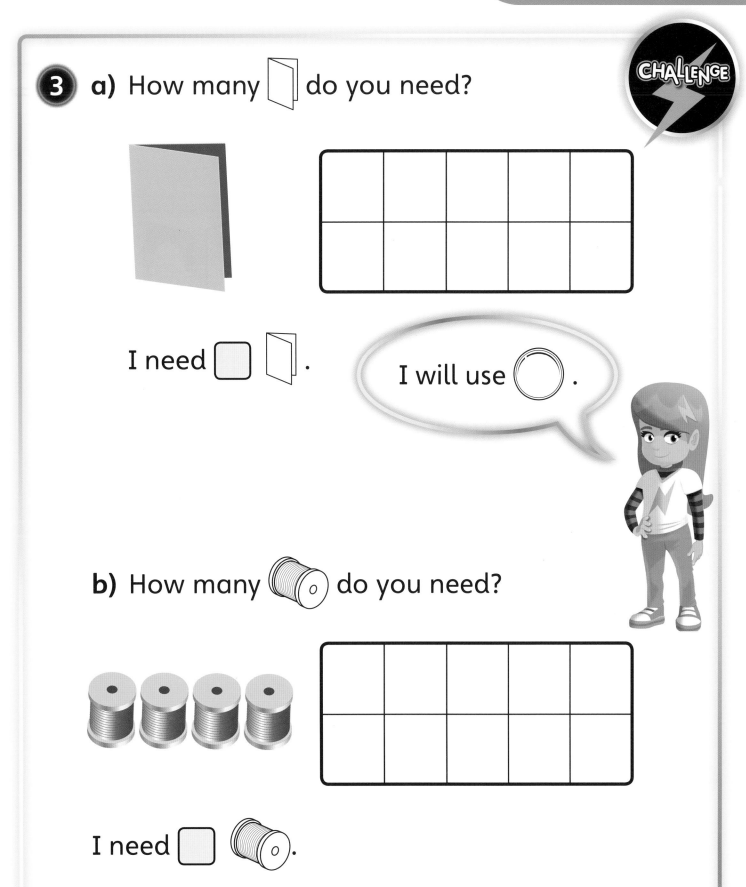 do you need?

I need ☐ ◻ .

I will use ◯ .

b) How many 🧵 do you need?

I need ☐ 🧵 .

→ Practice book 1A p9

Counting and writing numbers to 10

Discover

1 **a)** How many 🥫 are there?

b) Find two ways to write your answer.

Share

I used .

a)   10
ten

There are 10 .

You can use this **number track** to help.

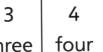
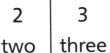

1	2	3	4	5	6	7	8	9	10
one	two	three	four	five	six	seven	eight	nine	ten

b) The number is 10.

The word is ten.

I wrote the number and the word.

17

Think together

1 Write how many 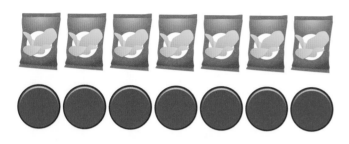 there are in numbers.

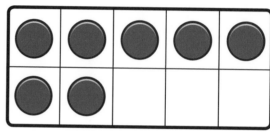

seven

There are ☐ .

2 Write how many 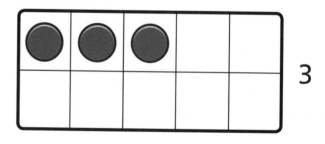 there are in words.

3

There are _____ .

3 How many are there?

How many are there?

Write the **digits** and the words.

There are ⬜ .

There are _____ .

There are ⬜ .

There are _____ .

They look different so they are not the same number.

I don't think you are correct. We could use ◯ to check.

19

Counting backwards from 10 to 0

Discover

10, 9, 8, 7, 6 ...

1 **a)** What number comes next?

b) How far back can you count?

Where do you stop counting?

Share

Is there a **pattern**?

a)

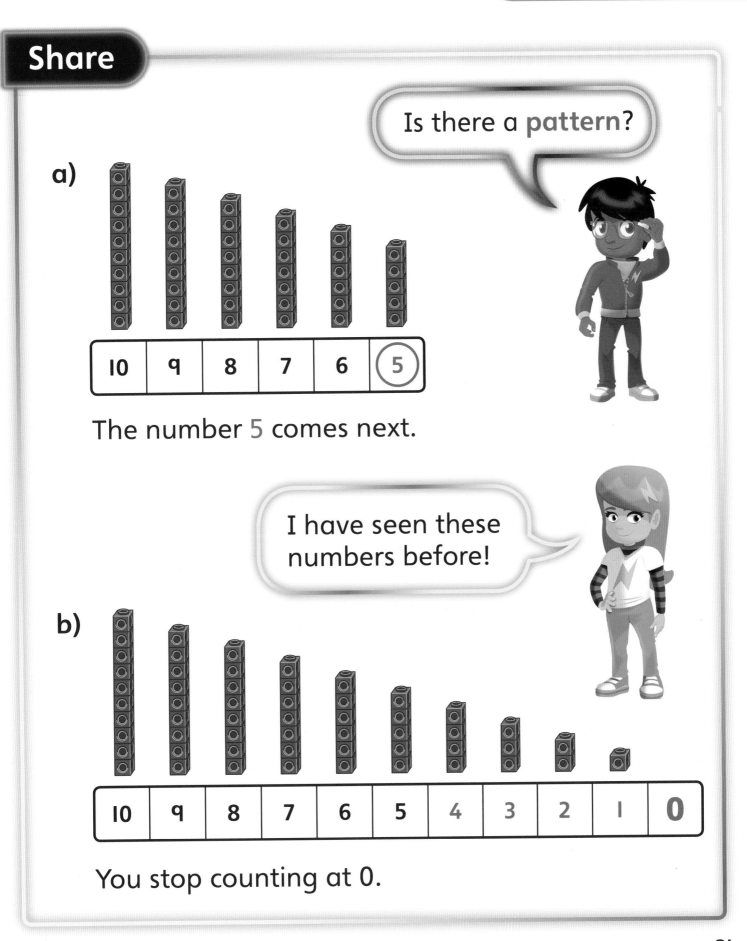

10	9	8	7	6	5

The number 5 comes next.

I have seen these numbers before!

b)

10	9	8	7	6	5	4	3	2	1	0

You stop counting at 0.

Think together

1 Complete the number track.

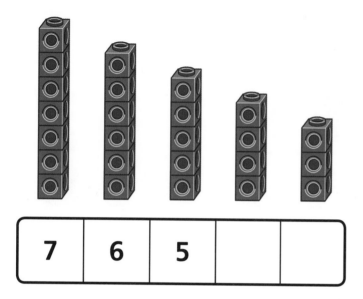

7	6	5		

2 Complete the number track.

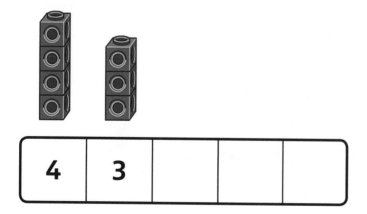

4	3			

3 **Count back** from 9 to 3.

9						

I wonder how many numbers there are from 9 to 3.

4 Count back from 8 to 1.

8							

If I can count back from 10 to 0, I can count back from 8 to 1!

→ Practice book 1A p15

Counting one more

Discover

1 **a)** There are 4 🦕 . **One more** 🦕 hatches.

How many 🦕 are there now?

b) One more 🦕 hatches.

How many 🦕 are there now?

24

Share

a)

1   2   3   4

I used 1  for each 🦕.

1   2   3   4   5

One more than 4 is 5.

There are 5 🦕 now.

b)

1   2   3   4   5

1   2   3   4   5   6

One more than 5 is 6.

There are 6 🦕 now.

Think together

1 What is one more than 2?

Use 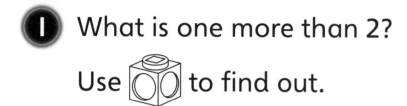 to find out.

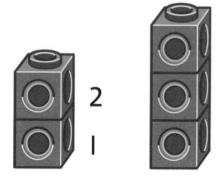

2

1

One more than 2 is ☐ .

2 What is one more than 3?

Use to find out.

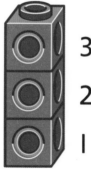

3

2

1

One more than 3 is ☐ .

3 **a)** One more than 8 is ☐ .

I counted 8 .
I took one more.
I counted again.

I started counting from 8.

b) 8 is one more than ☐ .

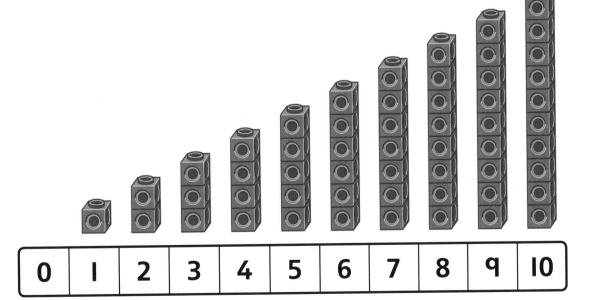

| 0 | 1 | 2 | 3 | 4 | 5 | 6 | 7 | 8 | 9 | 10 |

→ Practice book 1A p18

Counting one less

Discover

1 **a)** There are 7 chairs.

I chair is removed.

How many are left?

b) Another chair is removed. How many are left?

28

Share

I made a tower of cubes.

How can I make **one less**?

a)

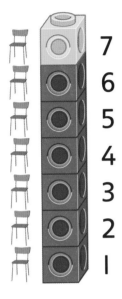

7
6
5
4
3
2
1

6
5
4
3
2
1

One less than 7 is 6. There are 6 chairs left.

b)

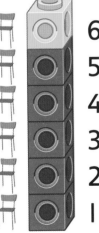

6
5
4
3
2
1

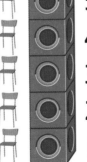

5
4
3
2
1

One less than 6 is 5. There are 5 chairs left now.

29

Think together

1 What is one less than 4?

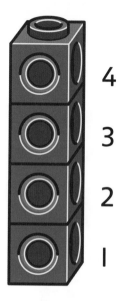

4

3

2

1

One less than 4 is ☐ .

2 What is one less than 3?

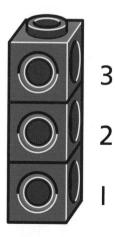

3

2

1

One less than 3 is ☐ .

3 **a)** One less than 9 is ☐ .

I counted 9 ⬜ .
I took one away.
I counted the ⬜ left.

b) 9 is one less than ☐ .

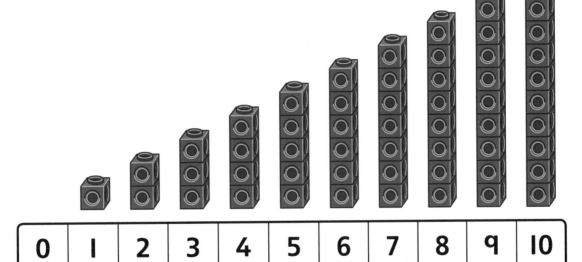

| 0 | 1 | 2 | 3 | 4 | 5 | 6 | 7 | 8 | 9 | 10 |

Is there a pattern
that makes it easier?

→ **Practice book 1A p21**

Comparing groups

Discover

1 **a)** Are there more 🚩 or more 🏰 ?

b) Can each person have a 🪣 ?

Share

I matched the 🏴 and the 🏰.

a)

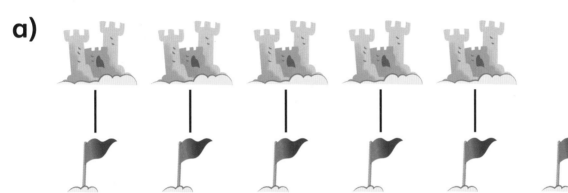

There are more 🏴.

b)

Each person cannot have a .

Think together

1. Are there more 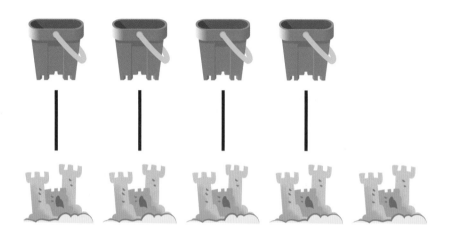 or more ... ?

There are more sandcastles.

2. Are there **fewer** people or fewer ... ?

There are fewer people.

3 Are there more ◯ or more ☐ ?

CHALLENGE

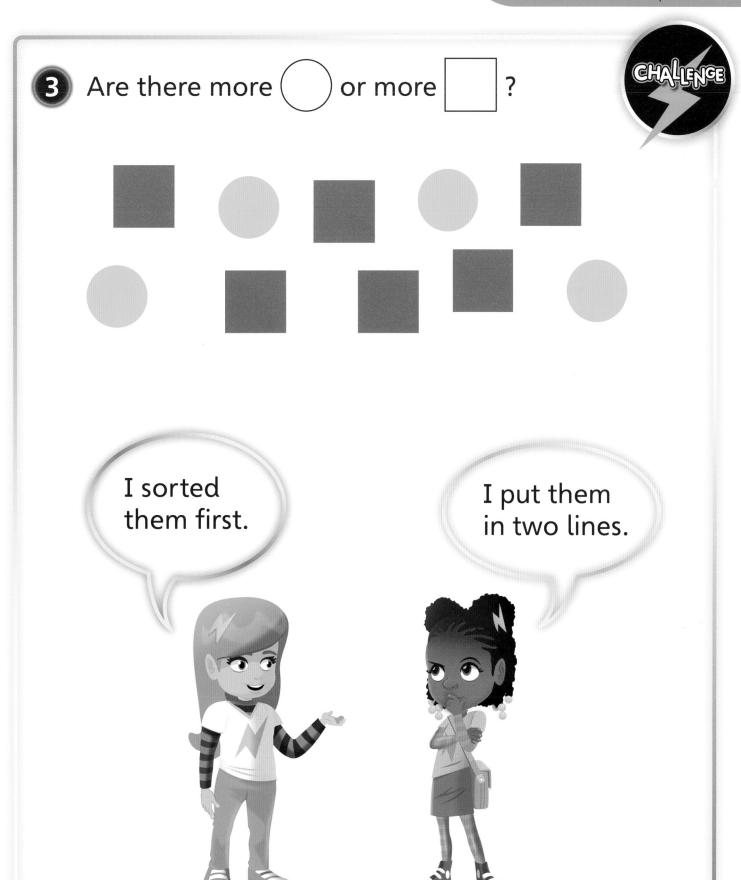

I sorted them first.

I put them in two lines.

→ **Practice book 1A p24**

Comparing numbers of objects

Discover

Tim   Lou   Anya

1 **a)** Who has more  ,Tim or Lou?

Who has fewer?

b) Who has more  , Tim or Anya?

36

Share

a)

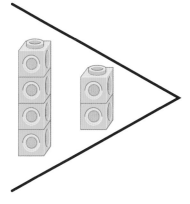 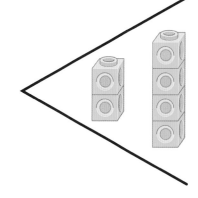

4 is **greater than** 2.   2 is **less than** 4.

4 > 2   2 < 4

Tim has more than Lou.

Lou has fewer than Tim.

b)

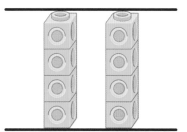

> means greater than or more than
>
> < means less than or fewer than
>
> = means equal to or the same as

4 is **equal to** 4.

4 = 4

Tim and Anya have an equal number of .

Think together

1 Complete using <, > or =.

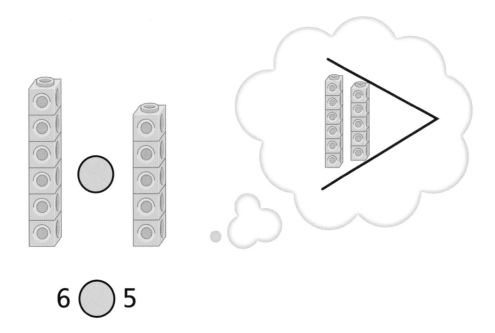

6 ◯ 5

2 Complete using <, > or =.

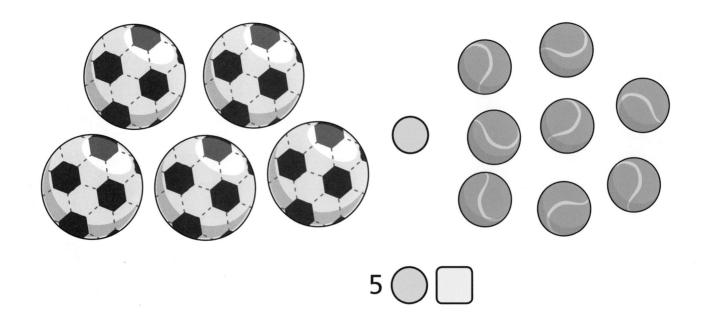

5 ◯ ▢

3 Draw more  than △ .

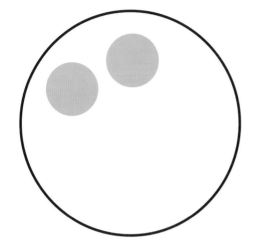 >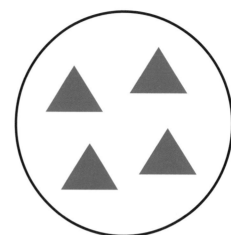

☐ > 4

I'll draw one more ◯ at a time and check.

Is there more than one answer?

→ Practice book 1A p27

Comparing numbers

Discover

1 **a)** Who has more , Bo or Jess?

b) Ted has fewer  than Bo. How many  could Ted have?

Share

a)

 >

I used  to represent 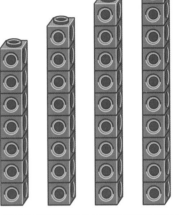.

7 > 4

| 0 | 1 | 2 | 3 | 4 | 5 | 6 | 7 | 8 | 9 | 10 |

7 > 4

Jess has more than Bo.

b)

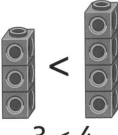 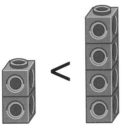

3 < 4   2 < 4   1 < 4   0 < 4

Ted could have 0, 1, 2 or 3 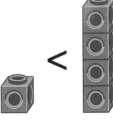.

Think together

1 Complete using <, > or =.

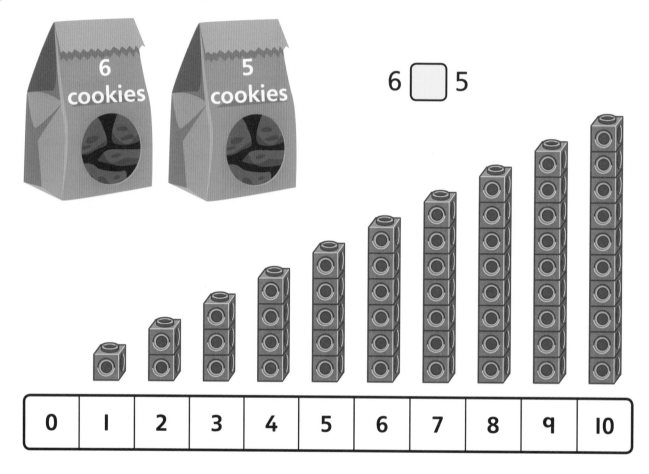

6 ☐ 5

| 0 | 1 | 2 | 3 | 4 | 5 | 6 | 7 | 8 | 9 | 10 |

2 Use < or > with the numbers to show who scored more.

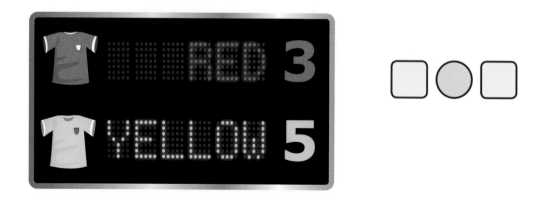

☐ ◯ ☐

3 Which of these numbers are greater than 7?

5

3

8

7

9

10

2

I used  to help me.

Should I choose 7?

→ Practice book 1A p30

Ordering objects and numbers

Discover

Kat   Em   Josh

1 **a)** Who has the **most** ⭐ ?

b) Order the children from the one who has the **least** ⭐ to the one who has the most.

Share

I will use  to compare them.

What does most mean?

a)

Em has the most .

b)

4	6	7
Kat	Josh	Em

45

Think together

1 How many 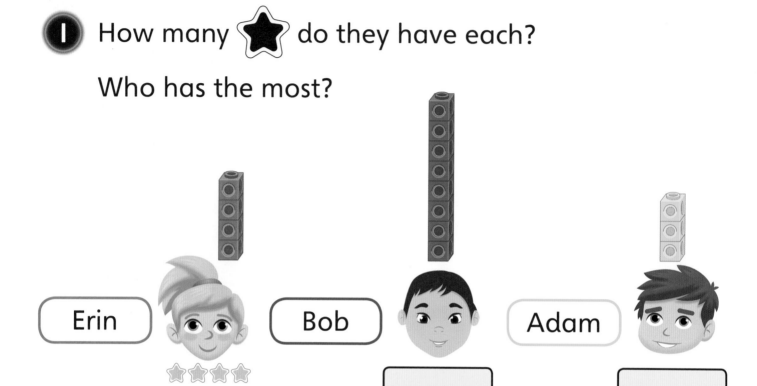 do they have each?

Who has the most?

Erin

Bob

Adam

2 Put the children in order, from the one who has the most  to the one who has the **fewest**.

_____, _____, _____.

3 **a)** Who rolled the **greatest** score?

b) Who rolled the least?

I rolled 4.

Jim

Eve

I rolled 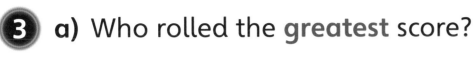 .

I rolled five.

Toby

I used towers of ⬚ to help me.

→ **Practice book 1A p33**

First, second, third...

Discover

1 **a)** What is the second activity?

b) What is the fourth activity?

Share

The children have to do four activities.

| first | second | third | fourth |
| 1st | 2nd | 3rd | 4th |

a) The second activity is throwing a bean bag into a bucket.

b) The fourth activity is jumping over some cones.

Think together

1 Who is the third child?

Luca   Ava   May   Carol   Ola

1st   2nd   3rd   4th   5th

2 What is on the fourth pizza?

chicken   peppers   cheese   meat   mushroom   olives   sweetcorn

1st   2nd

3 Who comes after the sixth person?

Nina Fay Milo Ali Ola Luca Jack Lola

1st   2nd

I think it is more than one person.

Do I circle the sixth person?

51

→ Practice book 1A p36

The number line

Discover

1 **a)** What numbers are missing?

b) What else is wrong?

Share

What numbers can you see?

It looks like a **number line**.

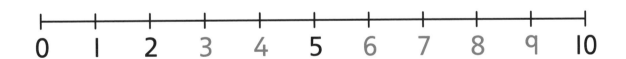

a) 4, 8 and 9 are missing.

b) 3 is upside-down.

6 and 7 are in the wrong order.

Think together

1 Complete the number line.

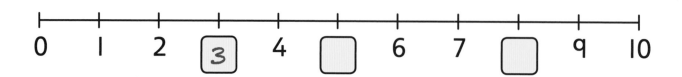

2 Which is greater, 4 or 7?

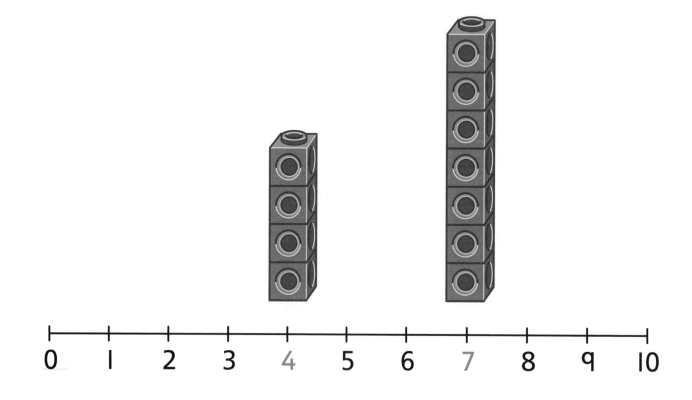

3 **a)** What is one more than 6?

b) What is one less than 6?

CHALLENGE

one more

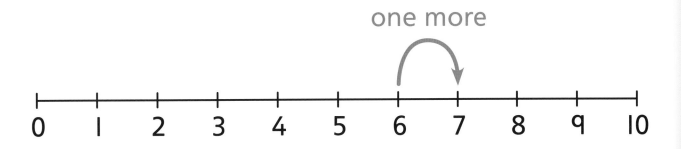
0 1 2 3 4 5 6 7 8 9 10

I like jumping on the number line, one more and one less!

Work out what is one more than 3 too.

55

→ Practice book 1A p39

End of unit check

Your teacher will ask you these questions.

1 What is the missing number?

_____ 1   2   3

A 4   **B** 1   **C** 0   **D** 5

2 What is the number?

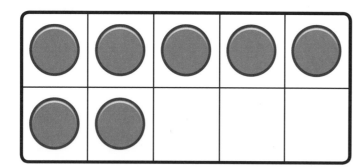

A 3   **B** 4   **C** 5   **D** 7

3 Demi is counting from 1 to 10. She says, 'four'.

What numbers come next?

A 3, 2, 1   **C** 5, 6, 7

B 5, 7, 6   **D** 4, 5, 6

4 Mary has 5 . Seb has 4 .

Which statement is correct?

A Seb has more than Mary.

B Mary has fewer than Seb.

C They both have the same amount of .

D Seb has fewer than Mary.

5 Which number is I more than 7?

   A 8   **B** 7   **C** 6   **D** 7I

Think!

Bea and Seth both have balloons.

Bea has .

Seth has  .

These words might help you.

balloon	I	**one**
more	3	**three**
less	5	**five**

57

→ Practice book 1A p42

Unit 2
Part-whole within 10

In this unit we will ...
- ⚡ Use the part-whole model
- ⚡ Write number sentences
- ⚡ Find different ways to make a number
- ⚡ Make number bonds
- ⚡ Compare number bonds

How could you put these flowers into 2 groups? Use 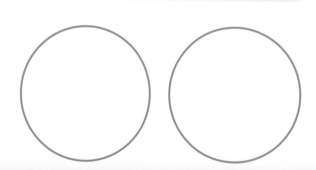 to help you!

Here are some maths words.
Have you used any of these before?

Groups   **Part-whole model**

Number sentence

How many different ways can
you make 5? Use  to help.

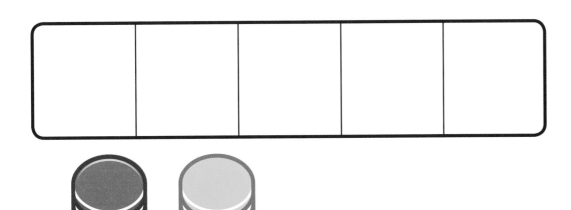

The part-whole model ❶

Discover

❶ **a)** How many children are there?

How many children are there in each **group**?

b) Complete the **part-whole model**.

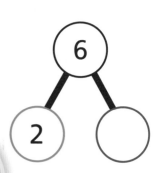

This is a part-whole diagram. It shows that 6 is the **whole**. 2 is a **part**. The other part is missing.

Share

a)

I drew the children.

I used counters.

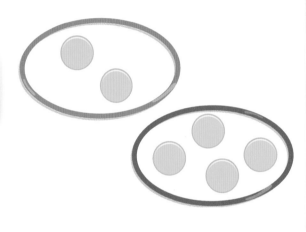

There are 6 children.

There are 2 children in the red hoop.

There are 4 children in the blue hoop.

b)

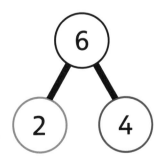

Think together

1 Now the children are in these 2 groups.

Show the groups and complete the part-whole diagram.

2 Is each 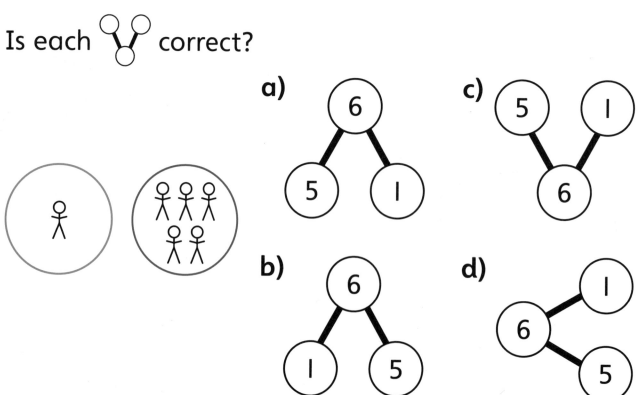 correct?

a)

6
5   1

c)

5   1
6

b)

6
1   5

d)

1
6
5

3 How could the children be put into two groups?

Is there just one way? Can you find a different way?

63

The part-whole model ②

Discover

1 **a)** There are 7 ✏.

How many are on the desk?

How many are in the tin?

Show or draw the groups.

b) Write this in a **number sentence**.

7 ✏ is **equal to** ☐ ✏ **plus** ☐ ✏ .

7 = ☐ + ☐

Share

a) There are 4  on the desk.

There are 3  in the tin.

I drew the  into 2 groups.

I put 4 in one circle and 3 in the other.

4   3

7

b) 7 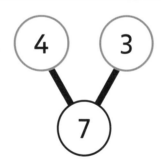 is equal to 4 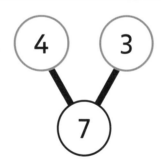 plus 3 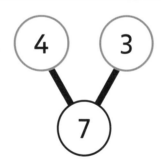 .

7 = 4 + 3

+ means plus
= means is equal to

65

Think together

1 **a)** Draw the 2 groups of .

 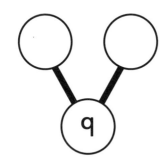

b) Complete the .

2 Find the mistakes.

a)

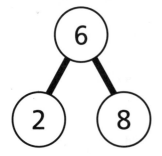

6 = 8 + 2

b)

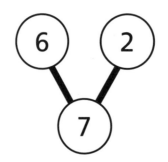

7 = 6 + 2

c)

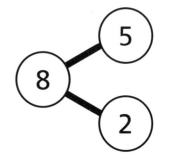

8 = 5 + 2

3 **a)** Put the beads into 2 groups.

b) Complete the .

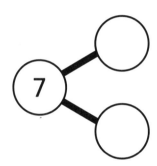

c) Write the number sentence.

☐ = ☐ + ☐

Are there other ways to group them?

67

→ Practice book 1A p47

Related facts – number bonds

Discover

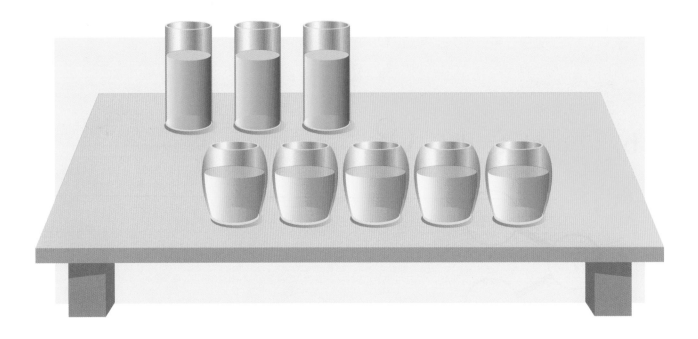

1 **a)** Put the 8 glasses into 2 groups.

Fill in the .

Write a number sentence.

b) Look at these number sentences.

What is the same? What is different?

$8 = 5 + 3$ $8 = 3 + 5$

$3 + 5 = 8$ $5 + 3 = 8$

Share

I can count the  and then the .

a)

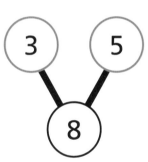

8 = 3 + 5

b) They all have the same three numbers: 8, 3, 5.

They all use the same symbols: + and =.

Two of the number sentences show 3 + 5.

The other two number sentences show 5 + 3.

Think together

1 Put the  and into groups.

Complete the .

Write a number sentence.

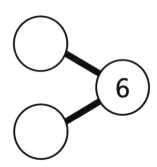

$\boxed{} + \boxed{} = 6$

2 Find the mistakes.

a)

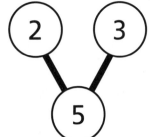

$\boxed{5} + \boxed{2} = \boxed{3}$

b)

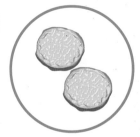 

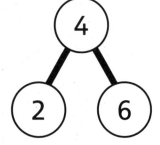

$\boxed{2} + \boxed{6} = \boxed{4}$

3 Look at the .

Fill in the numbers of flowers.

a)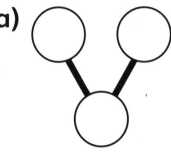

b) 5 + ☐ = 7

d) 2 + ☐ = ☐

c) ☐ = 5 + ☐

e) ☐ = 2 + ☐

Interesting. One  can make 4 additions.

Count carefully and put the numbers in the right place.

71

Finding number bonds

Discover

1 **a)** Use red and yellow ◯ to fill in the ▭▭▭▭ .

How many of each colour did you use?

▭▭▭▭▭

b) Can you find two more ways to fill in the ▭▭▭▭ ?

▭▭▭▭▭   ▭▭▭▭▭

Share

a)

I used I yellow  and

4 red  to fill in the ☐☐☐☐☐ .

b)

Here are two more ways I found.

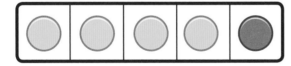   

Did you get the same?
How can we find all the ways?

Think together

1 Use ◯ to find all the ways to fill in the ☐☐☐☐ .

☐☐☐☐☐

2 How many different ways can you arrange 4 ◯ ?

Fill in the ☐☐☐☐ and the ⋎ .

a)

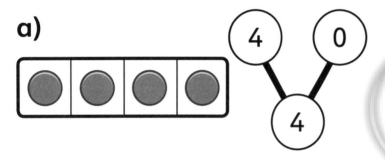

(4) (0)
(4)

Be organised with your method.

b)

(3) (1)

d)

c)

e)

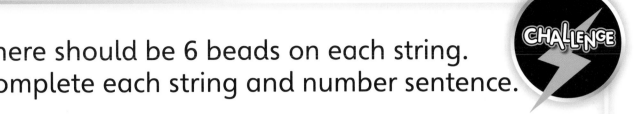

3 There should be 6 beads on each string.
Complete each string and number sentence.

$$6 = 6 + 0$$

$$6 = 1 + 5$$

$$6 = 2 + 4$$

$$6 = 3 + \boxed{}$$

$$6 = \boxed{} + \boxed{}$$

$$6 = \boxed{} + \boxed{}$$

75

→ Practice book 1A p53

Comparing number bonds

Discover

I am hiding 4 cubes.

I am also hiding 4 cubes.

Tom

Marta

1 a) Tom and Marta are playing a game.

Who has more ? How do you know?

b) Use the numbers and symbols to complete the number sentence.

$+$ $+$ $<$ | 1 | | 4 | | 4 | | 3 |

Share

a)

Marta and Tom are both hiding 4 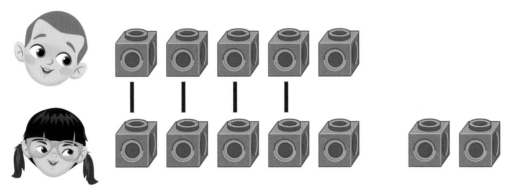. I know that whoever has more on the table has more in total.

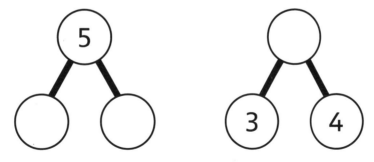

Marta has more  than Tom.

b)

$1 + 4 < 3 + 4$

Think together

1 Molly is hiding 6 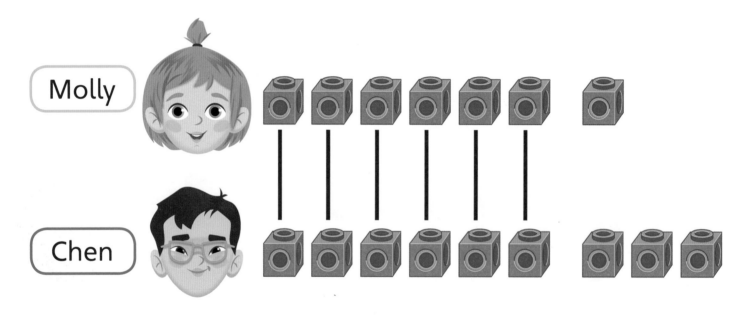. Chen is hiding 6 .

Molly has 1 on the table and Chen has 3

on the table.

Who has more ?

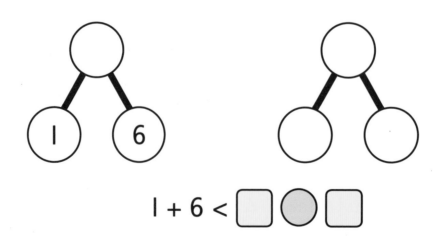

$$1 + 6 < \boxed{} \, \bigcirc \, \boxed{}$$

2 Molly is hiding 4 . Chen is hiding 3 .

Molly has 2 on the table and Chen has 2

on the table.

Who has more ?

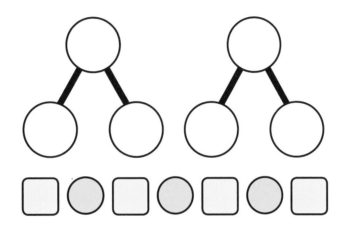

3 Replace ◯ with <, > or =.

$2 + 5$ ◯ $2 + 7$

$5 + 3$ ◯ $6 + 3$

$2 + 6$ ◯ $3 + 5$

$5 + 1$ ◯ $3 + 2$

Can you find a quick way of doing this?

79

→ Practice book 1A p56

End of unit check

Your teacher will ask you these questions.

 Which number completes the part-whole model?

A 5   C 3

B 14   D 4

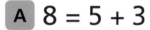

2 Which number sentence does not describe the part-whole model?

A 8 = 5 + 3   C 8 − 5 = 3

B 3 + 5 = 8   D 5 − 3 = 8

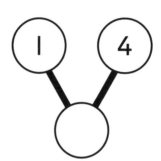

3 There are 7 children.

5 are boys and 2 are girls.

Which part-whole model describes the problem?

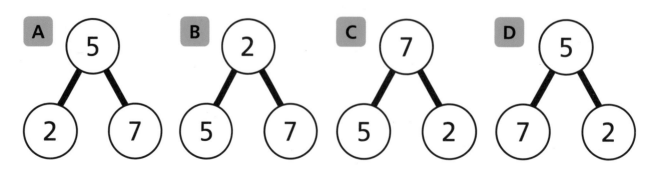

4 Which number sentence is a number bond to 4?

A $4 + 1 = 5$

B $4 = 3 + 4$

C $4 = 4 + 0$

D $4 = 4 + 4$

5 Toni has 5 red  and 2 blue .

Jamal has 4 red and 3 blue.

Which number sentence describes the ?

A $5 + 4 = 3 + 2$

B $2 + 4 = 5 + 3$

C $3 + 5 = 4 + 2$

D $5 + 2 = 4 + 3$

Think!

Can you put nine of these numbers into the part-whole models?

1   2   3   4   5   6   7   8   9   10

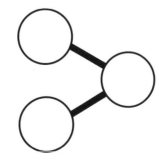

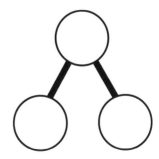

Is there more than one way?

81

→ Practice book 1A p59

Unit 3
Addition and subtraction within 10 ❶

In this unit we will ...
- ⚡ Add parts to find the whole
- ⚡ Find a missing part
- ⚡ Practise using number bonds
- ⚡ Find fact families
- ⚡ Solve word problems

Do you remember what this is called? Use it to find one more than 3.

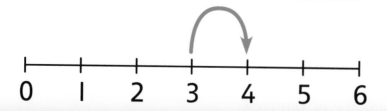

We will need some maths words. Which ones mean the same thing?

Altogether (say 'all-too-geth-er')

In total   **Plus**   **Add**

We need these too! Use them to make number sentences.

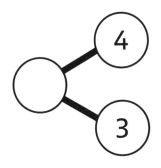

4

3

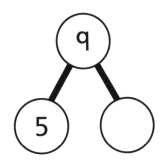

9

5

Finding the whole – adding together

Discover

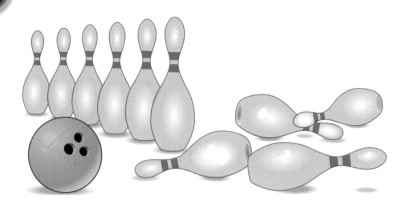

I **a)** How many 🎳 are left up?

How many 🎳 are knocked over?

How many 🎳 are there **altogether**?

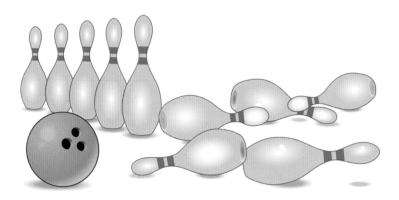

b) 1 more 🎳 is knocked over.

Now there are 5 🎳 left up and 5 🎳 knocked over.

How many 🎳 are there altogether?

Share

There are two parts.

To **add** we need to put the two parts together and count the whole.

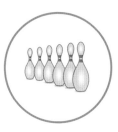 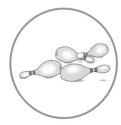

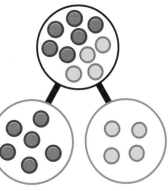

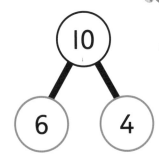

a) There are 6 left up.

There are 4 knocked over.

There are 10 altogether.

$$6 + 4 = 10$$

b) There are 5 left up.

There are 5 knocked over.

There are 10 altogether.

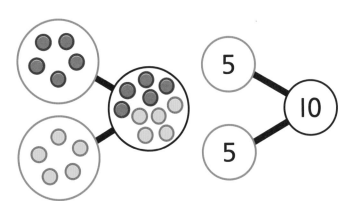

$$5 + 5 = 10$$

Think together

1 How many ⛳ are there **in total**?

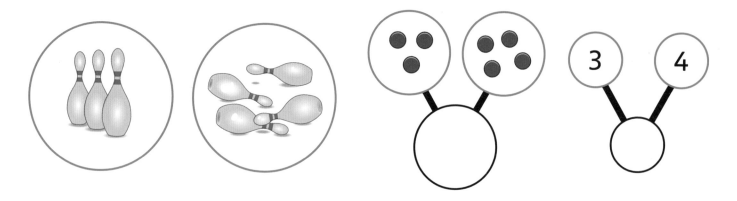

3 + 4 = ☐

There are ☐ ⛳ in total.

> In total also means the two parts added together.

2 How many ⛳ are there in total?

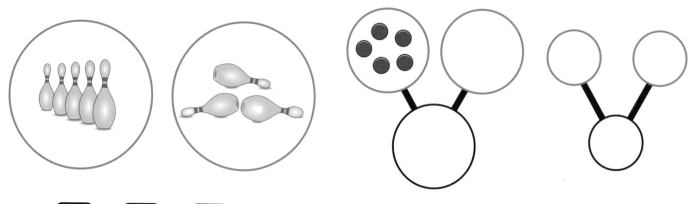

☐ + ☐ = ☐

There are ☐ ⛳ in total.

3 How many in total?
Use counters to help you.

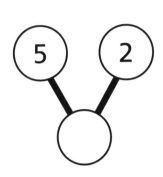

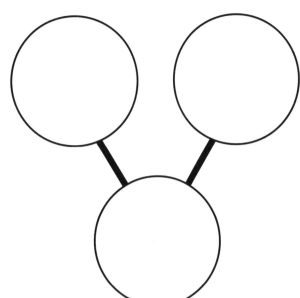

5 + 2 = ☐

Can you write
this addition
in other ways?
There are 3 more.

I know **plus** (+)
means add
the parts.

87

Finding the whole – adding more

Discover

1 **a)** 2  are added to the jar.

How many are in the jar now?

b) 3 more are added.

How many are in the jar now?

Share

a)

I will start with the 5 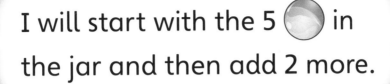 in the jar and then add 2 more.

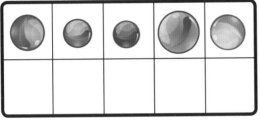 + =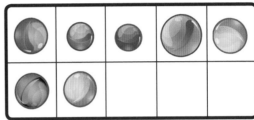

I can **count on** from 5. Start at 5 and then count on ... 6 ... 7.

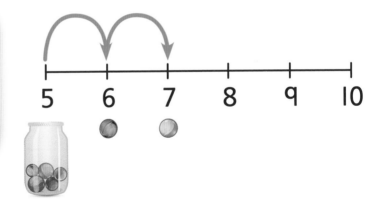

There are 5 ◯ in the jar.

2 more ◯ are added.

$5 + 2 = 7$

There are 7 ◯ in the jar now.

b) 7 + 3 = 10

There are 10 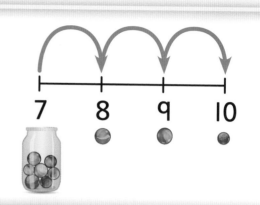 in the jar now.

Think together

1 There are 6 in the jar.

2 more go in the jar.

How many are in the jar now?

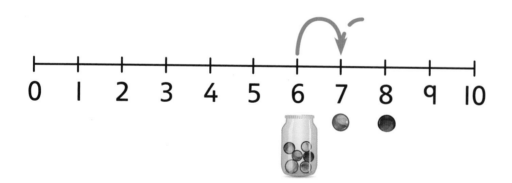

6 + ☐ = ☐

There are ☐ in the jar now.

2 There are 5 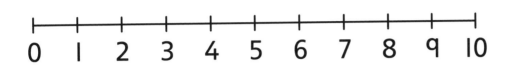 in the jar. 3 more 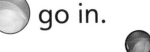 go in.

How many are in the jar now?

0   1   2   3   4   5   6   7   8   9   10

☐ + ☐ = ☐

There are ☐ 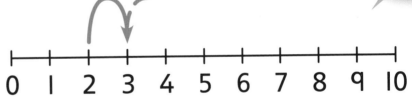 in the jar now.

3 Use a number line to work out 2 + 7 = ☐

CHALLENGE

I know that
2 + 7 = 7 + 2.

0   1   2   3   4   5   6   7   8   9   10

0   1   2   3   4   5   6   7   8   9   10

Which number should you count on from? Why?

91

→ Practice book 1A p64

Finding a part

Discover

Snacks
– I per
person

I There are 8 children.

a) 5 children each get an ⬤.

How many children get a 🍌?

b) Tomorrow 2 children will get a 🍌,

2 will get a 🍐 and the rest will get an ⬤.

How many children will get an ⬤?

92

Share

a) 5  + ☐ 🍌 = 8

Use 1 ◯ for each piece of fruit.

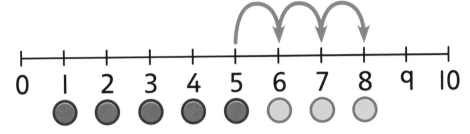

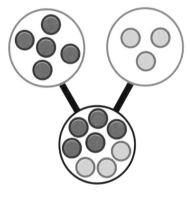 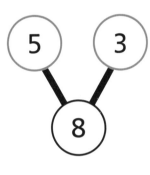

5 + 3 = 8

There are 3 🍌.

b) 2 🍌 + 2 🍐 = 4 ⟶ 4 + 4 🍎 = 8

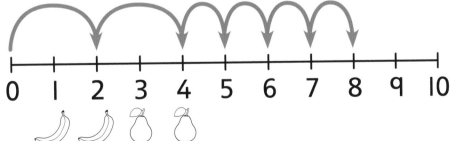 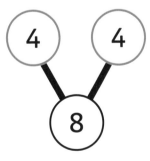

There are 4 🍎.

Think together

1 There are 8 pieces of fruit altogether.

How many  are there?

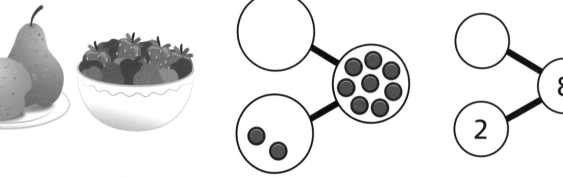

$2 + \boxed{} = 8$

There are $\boxed{}$.

2 There are 9 pens and 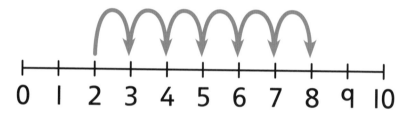 altogether.

How many 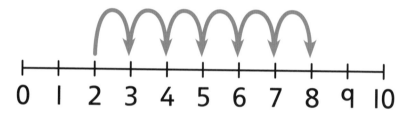 are there?

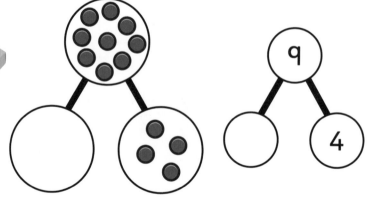

$4 + \boxed{} = 9$

There are $\boxed{}$  .

3 Find the **missing part.**

Use the  and number line to help you.

a) $5 + \boxed{} = 7$

$\boxed{} + 5 = 7$

b) $3 + \boxed{} = 7$

$\boxed{} + 3 = 7$

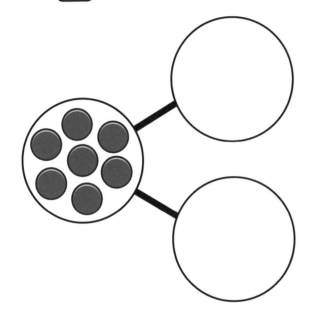

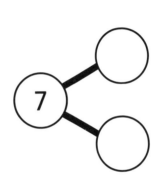

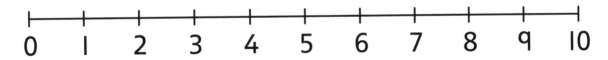

Do I need to work out all four answers?

95

→ **Practice book 1A p67**

Finding and making number bonds

Discover

1 **a)** There are 10 in total.

7 are left up.

How many did Tom hit?

b) Anna hits 5 .

How many are left up?

Share

a)

I can start at 7 and count on.

 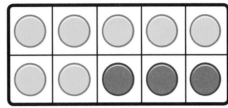 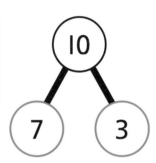

There are 10 in total.

7 are left up.

$7 + 3 = 10$

Tom hit 3 .

b)

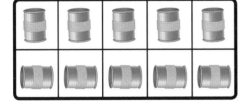 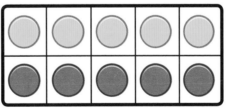 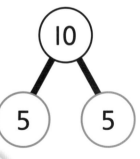

Anna hits 5 .

$5 + 5 = 10$

There are 5 left up.

This time we need to start at 5.

Think together

1 How many 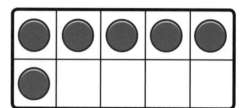 were hit?

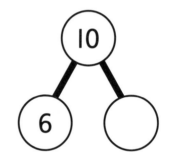

6 + ☐ = 10

☐  were hit.

2 How many 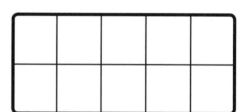 were hit?

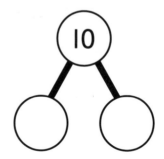

☐ + ☐ = 10

☐  were hit.

3 Complete the diagrams and number sentences.

$10 + 0 = 10$

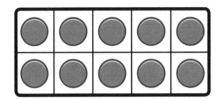

$9 + 1 = 10$

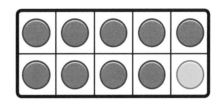

$8 + \boxed{} = \boxed{}$

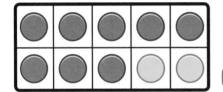

$7 + \boxed{} = \boxed{}$

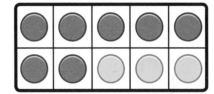

$6 + \boxed{} = \boxed{}$

$5 + \boxed{} = \boxed{}$

I worked in order.

I remember $5 + 5 = 10$.

→ Practice book 1A p70

Finding addition facts

Discover

We are planting seeds.

1 **a)** There are 6 🌼 in the tub.

Each child plants one seed.

How many 🌼 will grow in total?

b) After I week there are 7 🌼 in the tub.

How many seeds are still to grow?

Share

a)

I can show it on a ☐☐☐☐☐ .

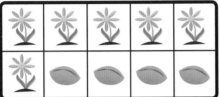 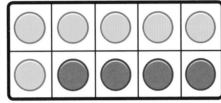 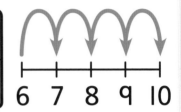

There are 6 🌼 and 4 seeds.

6 + 4 = 10

10 🌼 will grow in total.

I know that
6 + 4 = 10.
I remember these
numbers from
last lesson.

b) There are 7 🌼 .

7 + ☐ = 10

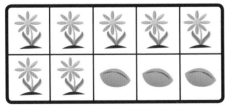 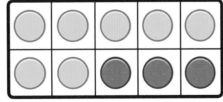 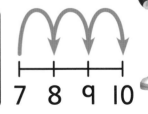

7 + 3 = 10

3 seeds are still to grow.

Think together

1 There should be 10 in total.

How many are missing?

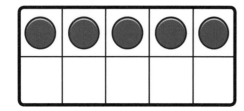

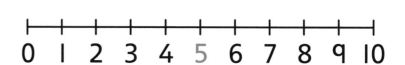

5 + ☐ = 10   ☐  are missing.

2 There should be 10  in total.

How many are missing?

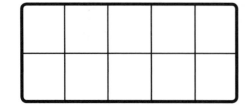

☐ + ☐ = ☐   ☐ 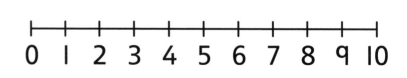 are missing.

3 How many are there in total?

Can you write this in two ways?

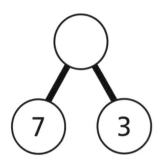

7   3

☐ + ☐ = 10

☐ + ☐ = 10

If I know 8 + 2 then
I also know 2 + 8.
Can this help me
with the question?

→ Practice book 1A p73

Solving word problems – addition

Discover

I **a)** Jack has 4 🐕 and Liz has 4 🐕.

How many 🐕 are there altogether?

b) Can you use the picture to find I + 3?

Show this using a 🔗.

Share

I can just count them.

I think adding is quicker.
I will use a or a $\underset{0 \quad 5 \quad 10}{\vdash}$.

a)

Use I ⬤ for each  or person.

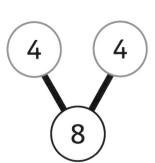

4 + 4 = 8

There are 8 in total.

b)

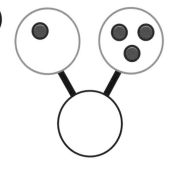

1 + 3 = 4

There are 4 people on the  .

Think together

1 There are 6 🥧 in the box.

There are 3 🥧 on the plate.

How many 🥧 are there altogether?

6 Jam Tarts

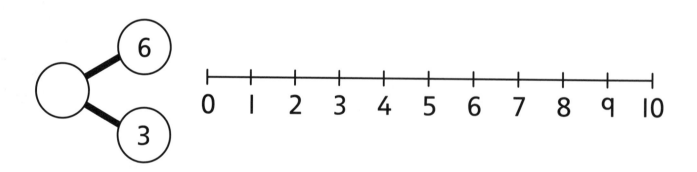

0 1 2 3 4 5 6 7 8 9 10

◻ + ◻ = ◻

There are ◻ 🥧 altogether.

106

2 ☐ girls are on the  .

☐ boys are on the ⬡ .

How many children are there altogether?

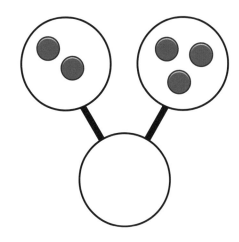

Find two ways to show this fact.

☐ + ☐ = ☐   ☐ + ☐ = ☐

There are ☐ children altogether.

3 Look at the park on p104.
Can you see any other **number stories**?
Ask a friend.

CHALLENGE

How many number stories can you find?

Can you find a story no one else has seen?

107

→ Practice book 1A p76

End of unit check

Your teacher will ask you these questions.

1 Gabe has 5 . Tia has 4 .

Which number line shows the total

number of ?

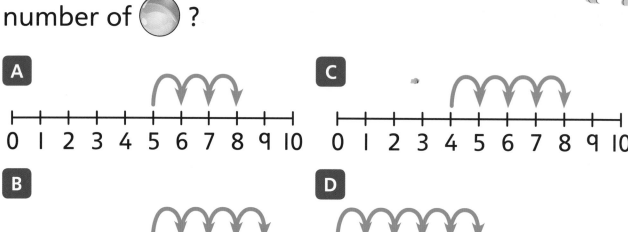

A

0 1 2 3 4 5 6 7 8 9 10

C

0 1 2 3 4 5 6 7 8 9 10

B

0 1 2 3 4 5 6 7 8 9 10

D

0 1 2 3 4 5 6 7 8 9 10

2 Which number sentence gives the total?

A 4 + 2 = 6   **C** 6 + 2 = 8

B 2 + 4 = 4   **D** 2 + 6 = 0

3 3 + ☐ = 7

What is the missing number?

A 7   **B** 10   **C** 4   **D** 0

108

4 Which does not add to 10?

A 5 5   B 0 10   C 1 0   D 8 2

4 Which number sentence works out how many in total?

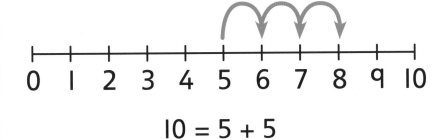

A $2 + 7 = 9$

B $5 + 4 = 8$

C $9 = 5 + 4$

D $9 = 6 + 3$

Think!

Choose an odd one out. Explain your choice.

$$10 = 5 + 5$$

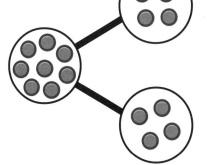

These words might help you.

part   whole   total

add   number   cube

109

→ Practice book 1A p79

Unit 4
Addition and subtraction within 10 ②

In this unit we will …
- ⚡ Take away to find how many are left
- ⚡ Subtract by breaking the whole into parts
- ⚡ Discover related number facts
- ⚡ Comparing additions and subtractions
- ⚡ Find the difference
- ⚡ Solve word problems

We have used this before. Which ⚭ shows the problem correctly?

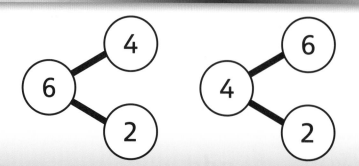

These maths words and phrases will help us. Do you know any of these?

How many are left?   **Take away**

Subtract   **Count backwards**

How many more   **How many fewer**

Difference

How can you use  to find which is greater?

Subtraction – how many are left? ❶

Discover

Amy

❶ **a)** Amy has 6 ⬭.

I ⬭ floats away.

How many ⬭ are left?

b) One ⬭ pops. **How many are left?**

Share

Use I ◯ for each ◯.

a)

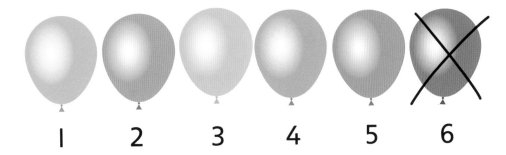

1   2   3   4   5   6

There are 6 ◯.

I floats away.

There are 5 ◯ left.

I just counted the ◯ left.

b)

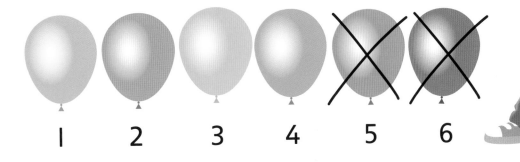

1   2   3   4   5   6

One ◯ pops.

There are 4 ◯ left.

Think together

1 There are 7  in total.

I  pops.

How many  are left?

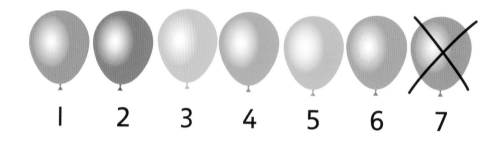

1 2 3 4 5 6 7

There are ☐  left.

2 2 of these  pop. How many balloons are left?

There are ☐  left.

3 How many 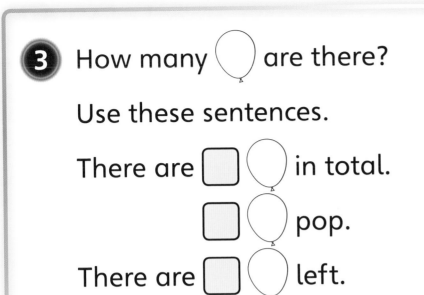 are there?

Use these sentences.

There are ☐ ◯ in total.

☐ ◯ pop.

There are ☐ ◯ left.

a)

b)

CHALLENGE

I can see a pattern in the answers.

c)

d)

115

Subtraction – how many are left? ②

Discover

1 **a)** How many children are in the classroom?

How many children leave the classroom?

How many children are left in the classroom?

b) Four more children leave the classroom.

How many children are left in the classroom now?

Share

a)

 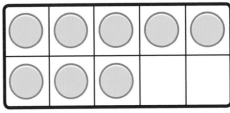

8 children are in the classroom.

2 children leave the classroom.

8 − 2 = 6

☐ children are left in the classroom.

b)

 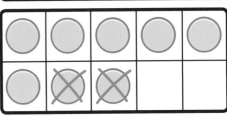

Four more children leave the classroom.

6 − 4 = 2

There are ☐ children left in the classroom.

Think together

1 There are 9 children.

3 children leave.

9 – ⬜ = ⬜

There are ⬜ children left.

2 There are 7 children.

Some children leave.

How many are left?

⬜ – ⬜ = ⬜

There are ⬜ children left.

3

There are ☐ ◯ in **total**.

☐ ◯ are **taken away**.

☐ ◯ ☐ = ☐

There are ☐ ◯ **left**.

> **Subtract can mean take away.**

What does − 4 mean?

Which number shows the number that you start with?

119

Subtraction – breaking apart ①

Discover

① **a)** There are 9 🚗 in the car park.

Ava washes 4 🚗 .

How many are still dirty?

b) Ava washes 2 more 🚗 .

How many are still dirty now?

Share

a) There are 9  in the car park.

Ava washes 4 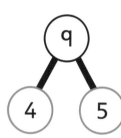.

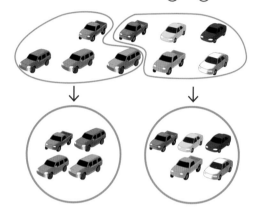

$9 - 4 = 5$

5 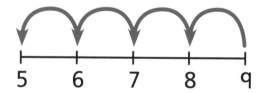 are still dirty.

5   6   7   8   9

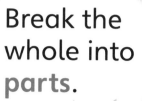

9
4   5

I can check the answer by counting back.

b) Ava washes 2 more 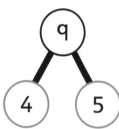.

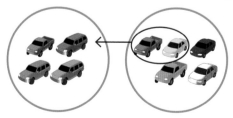

9
6   3

There are 3 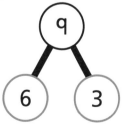 still dirty.

Think together

1 There are 8 🚗 in the car park.

Hugo washes 5 🚗 .

How many cars are still dirty?

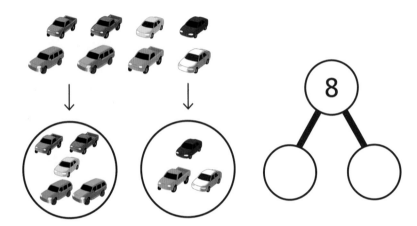

$8 - 5 = \boxed{}$

$\boxed{}$ 🚗 are still dirty.

2 There are 7 🚗 in the car park.

Hugo washes 5 🚗 .

How many cars are still dirty?

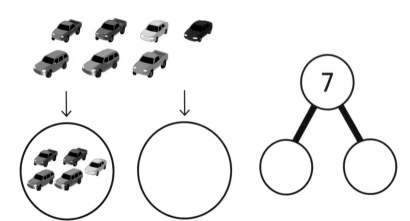

$7 - \boxed{} = \boxed{}$

$\boxed{}$ cars are still dirty.

3 **a)** There are 6 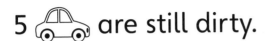 in a car park.

Ava washes some of the 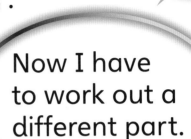.

5 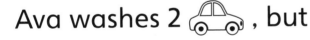 are still dirty.

How many 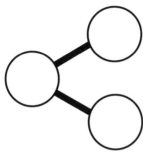 did Ava wash?

> Now I have to work out a different part.

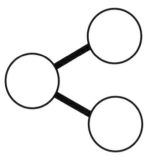

b) There are some  in a car park.

Ava washes 2 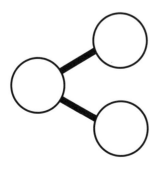, but

6 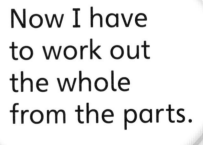 are still dirty.

How many cars are there in total?

> Now I have to work out the whole from the parts.

123

→ Practice book 1A p87

Subtraction – breaking apart ❷

Discover

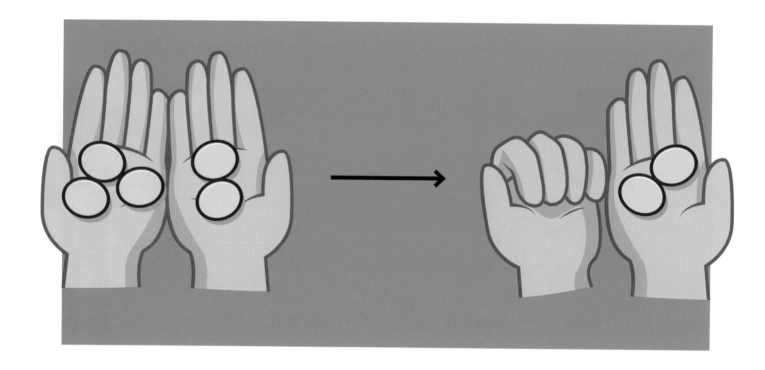

I **a)** There are 5 ◯ in total.

There are 2 ◯ in the ✋.

How many ◯ are hidden in the ✊?

b) How can you check?

Share

I will just guess because I cannot see them.

I can work out the parts.

a) There are 5 ◯ in total.

There are 2 ◯ in the .

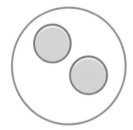

?

5 − 2 = 3

$\boxed{5} - \boxed{2} = \boxed{}$

There are 3 ◯ hidden in the ✊.

b) There are 2 ◯ in .

There are 3 ◯ in the ✊.

2 + 3 = 5

To check a **subtraction** you can do an **addition**.

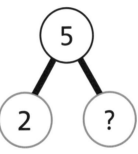

125

Think together

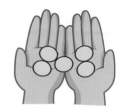

1 There are 5 ◯ in total.

There are 4 ◯ in the .

How many ◯ are hidden in the ?

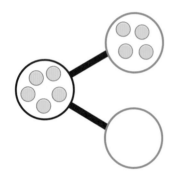   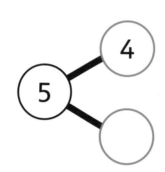

5 − 4 = ☐

There is ☐ ◯ hidden in the 🖐.

2 There are 7 ◯ in total.

There are ☐ ◯ in the 🖐.

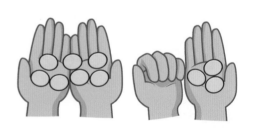

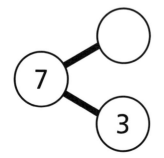

7 − 3 = ☐

There are ☐ ◯ hidden in the 🖐.

126

3 There are 6  in total.

How many are hidden under the cloth?

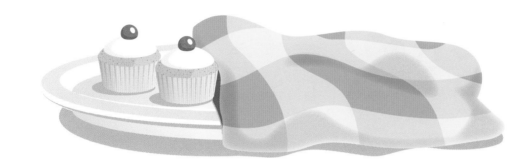

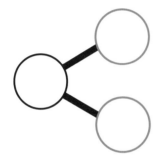 $6 - 2 = \boxed{}$

There are $\boxed{}$ hidden under the cloth.

I can use .

I can draw 1 ◯ for each .

127

→ **Practice book 1A p90**

Related facts – addition and subtraction ❶

Discover

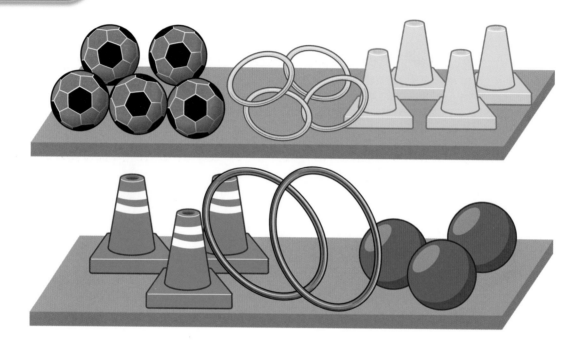

❶ **a)** How many ?

How many ?

How many balls in total? How can you check?

b) I bursts.

How many in total now?

Show 2 ways to find this.

Share

a)

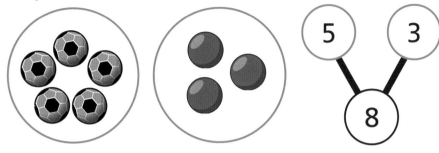

$5 + 3 = 8$ $3 + 5 = 8$

There are 8 balls in total.

You **add** to find the total.

5 + 3 gives the same answer as 3 + 5. You can add in any order and you will get the same answer!

b)

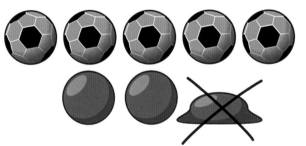

$5 + 2 = 7$

$2 + 5 = 7$

There are 7 balls in total.

129

Think together

1 There are 7 cones in total.

How many ? How many ?

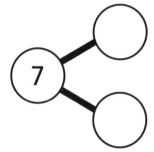

□ – □ = □

□ – □ = □

2 Complete the **number sentences** for the hoops.

□ + □ = □

□ + □ = □

□ – □ = □

□ – □ = □

One of the number sentences shows how many small hoops there are.

Which one shows this fact?

3 There are 4 balls in total.

3 are rugby balls.

How many tennis balls are there?

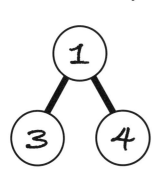

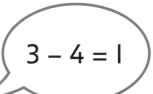
3 – 4 = 1

What mistakes has she made?

What is wrong with the diagram?

What does – 4 mean?

131

→ Practice book 1A p93

Related facts – addition and subtraction ❷

Discover

❶ **a)** Leon throws 6 rings.

2 rings miss.

How many does he score?

b) How many different number sentences can you find to show this fact?

Share

a) There are 6 rings in total.

2 rings miss.

6 – 2 = 4

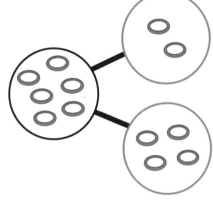

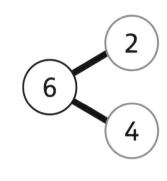

Leon scores 4 rings.

b)

I got 4 number sentences.

6 – 2 = 4

6 – 4 = 2

2 + 4 = 6

4 + 2 = 6

I found a different way to write them.

4 = 6 – 2

2 = 6 – 4

6 = 2 + 4

6 = 4 + 2

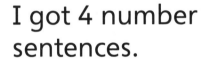

There are 8 different number sentences that show this fact.

Think together

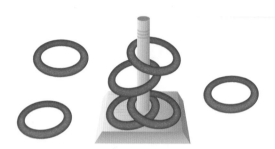

1 Leon throws 7 rings.

He scores 4. How many miss?

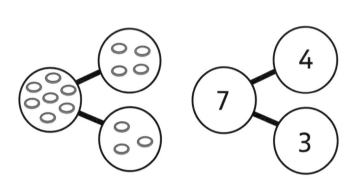

$7 - 4 = \boxed{}$

$\boxed{} = 7 - 4$

$\boxed{}$ rings miss.

2 How many rings are there in total?
Find the number sentences to show this fact.

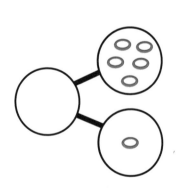

$\boxed{} + \boxed{} = \boxed{}$

$\boxed{} + \boxed{} = \boxed{}$

$\boxed{} - \boxed{} = \boxed{}$

$\boxed{} - \boxed{} = \boxed{}$

3 Find all the number sentences.

  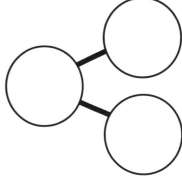

$9 = \boxed{} + 5$

$4 + \boxed{} = 9$

$9 = 5 + \boxed{}$

$\boxed{} + \boxed{} = 9$

$5 = \boxed{} - \boxed{}$

$\boxed{} - \boxed{} = 5$

□ ○ □ ○ □   □ ○ □ ○ □

I can write the same fact in different ways.

135

→ **Practice book 1A p96**

Subtraction – counting back

Discover

1 **a)** Maya has to jump 3 times $\underset{\wedge\wedge\wedge}{\boxed{3}}$.

What number will she land on?

b) Maya jumps 2 more times $\underset{\wedge\wedge}{\boxed{2}}$.

Where does she land?

Share

I can **count** backwards: 9, 8, 7, 6, 5, 4, 3, 2, 1.

Have you stopped at the right number?

a)

8...7...6

$9 - 3 = 6$

 lands on 6.

b)

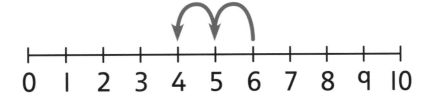

 starts on 6.

She jumps 2 more ...5...4. $6 - 2 = 4$

Maya lands on 4.

Think together

1 Where does Maya land?

$6 - 1 = \boxed{}$

What is 1
less than 6?

I less than 6 is $\boxed{}$.

2 Where does Maya land?

$5 - 2 = \boxed{}$

2 less than 5 is $\boxed{}$.

138

CHALLENGE

3   3 –  = 0

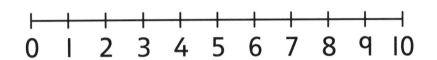
| | | | 3 | 4 | 5 |

0   1   2   3   4   5   6   7   8   9   10

2 –  = 0

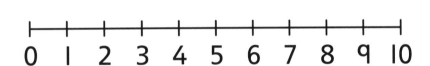
| | 2 | 3 | 4 | 5 |

0   1   2   3   4   5   6   7   8   9   10

1 –  = 0

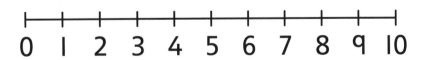
| 1 | 2 | 3 | 4 | 5 |

0   1   2   3   4   5   6   7   8   9   10

I can write the numbers.

I think I can see a pattern.

139

→ Practice book 1A p99

Subtraction – finding the difference

Discover

1 **a)** **How many more** children are there in the back row?

b) **How many fewer** children are there in the front row?

Share

I need to line up the ◯ so that I can compare and find the **difference**.

You can **count on** or count back to find the difference.

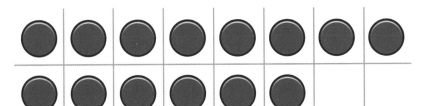

a)

There are 2 more children in the back row.

If I know how many more then do I know how many fewer?

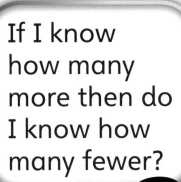

b)

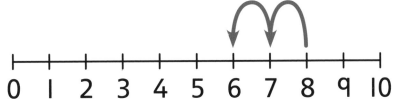

There are 2 fewer children in the front row.

Think together

1 How many more children are there in the front row?

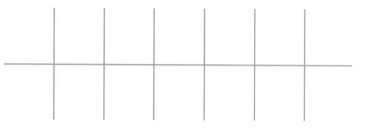

⬚ – ⬚ = ⬚

There are ⬚ more children in the front row.

2 How many fewer children are there in the front row?

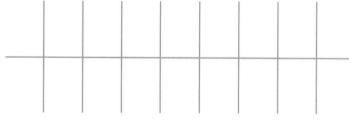

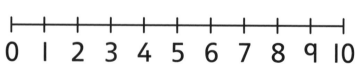

⬚ – ⬚ = ⬚

There are ⬚ fewer children in the front row.

142

3 **a)** How many more children are there in the back row?

CHALLENGE

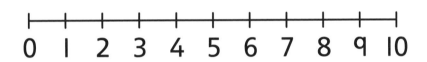

0 1 2 3 4 5 6 7 8 9 10

☐ ◯ ☐ = ☐

There are ☐ more children in the back row.

I've spotted a pattern.

b) How many fewer children are there in the front row?

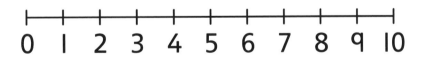

0 1 2 3 4 5 6 7 8 9 10

☐ ◯ ☐ = ☐

There are ☐ fewer children in the front row.

Is it always the same?

143

→ Practice book 1A p102

Solving word problems – subtraction

Discover

1 **a)** Can you see a story for 7 – 3?

b) Work out 7 – 3.

Share

Is this a take away?

I am searching for 7 things.

a) There are 7 🍦 in total.

3 of them have melted.

b)

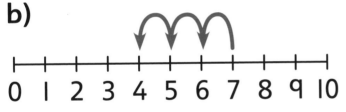

0 1 2 3 4 5 6 7 8 9 10

$7 - 3 = 4$

145

Think together

1 There are 10 people in total.

5 people are wearing  .

How many people are not wearing  ?

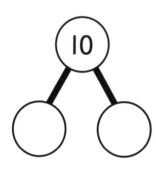

$10 - 5 = \boxed{}$

> Use ◯ to show the people.

$\boxed{}$ people are not wearing  .

2 How many more people are going into Screen 1 than Screen 2?

Screen 1

Screen 2

$\boxed{} - \boxed{} = \boxed{}$

There are $\boxed{}$ more people in the line for Screen 1.

3 Make up your own subtraction stories.

What different subtractions can you see?

CHALLENGE

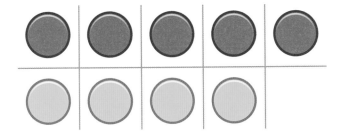

I can see a take away and I can find a difference.

147

→ **Practice book 1A p105**

Comparing additions and subtractions ❶

Discover

❶ **a)** Can everyone go on the ride together?

b) How many people are left?

Share

a)

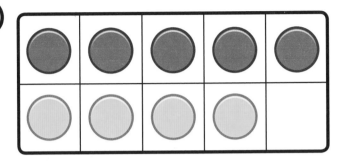

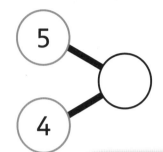

5 + 4 = 9

9 is greater than 8.

9 > 8

They cannot all get on together.

Use I 〇 for each person.

b)

ROLLER COASTER

Maximum 8 people

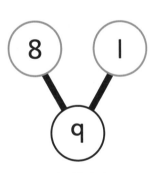

9 − 8 = 1

There is I person left.

Is there a better way?

Think together

1 There are 9 people waiting for the ride.

3 people leave.

a) How many people are left waiting for the ride?

☐ – ☐ = ☐

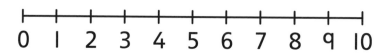

0 1 2 3 4 5 6 7 8 9 10

b) Can they all go on the ride together?

☐ is _____ than ☐.

☐ ◯ ☐

They _____ all go on the ride together.

2 How many people are there in total?

Can they all go on the ride together?

 = ☐

They _____ all go on the ride together.

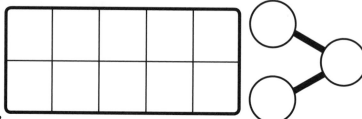

3 There are **6** people waiting for the ride.

I person leaves.

Can the people left waiting all go on the ride?

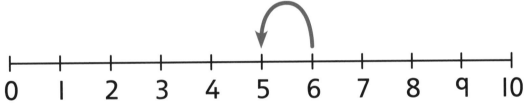

0 1 2 3 4 5 6 7 8 9 10

Show ⬜ – ⬜ ⚪ ⬜

They _____ all go on the ride.

> I do not think that I needed to do a subtraction. I can see it will be less.

151

Comparing additions and subtractions ❷

Discover

Emily

Nate

❶ How many ▯ does each waiter have?

Which waiter has the most ▯?

Share

Use I cube for each .

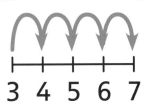

Emily

3 + 4 = 7

3 4 5 6 7

Nate

3 + 3 = 6

3 4 5 6 7

7 > 6

Emily has the most .

I worked out how much each waiter had and compared the numbers.

Emily   Nate

 +  >

③ + 4 > ③ + 3

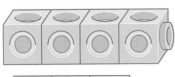

Emily has the most .

I compared the trays. each waiter had a tray with 3  so I just compared the other tray.

Think together

I Which waiter has more 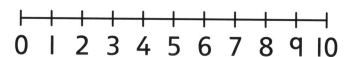, Emily or Nate?

 Emily

$$\boxed{} + \boxed{} = \boxed{}$$

 Nate

$$\boxed{} + \boxed{} = \boxed{}$$

$$\boxed{} + \boxed{} \bigcirc \boxed{} + \boxed{}$$

_____ has more 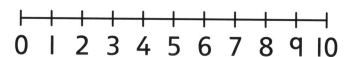.

2 Are there more 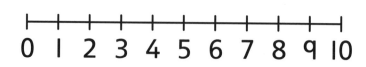 or left?

$$\boxed{} - \boxed{} \bigcirc \boxed{} - \boxed{}$$

There are more _____ .

154

3 Compare the number of drinks each person has. Compare in two ways.

CHALLENGE

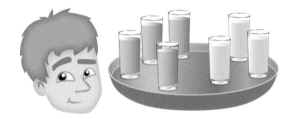

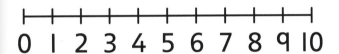

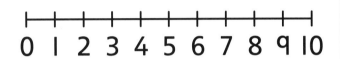

⬜ ⚪ ⬜ = ⬜   ⬜ ⚪ ⬜ = ⬜

I think you need to add for one and subtract for the other.

I will try to compare the number of drinks without working out the answers.

155

→ Practice book 1A p111

Solving word problems – addition and subtraction

Discover

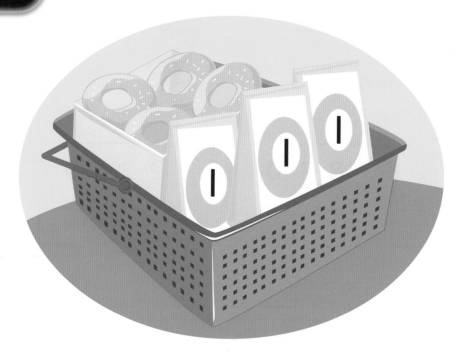

1 a) How many 🍩 are there in total?

b) 2 🍩 are eaten.

How many are left?

Share

a)

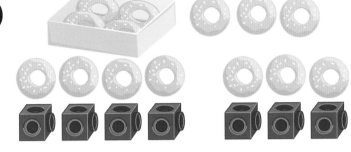

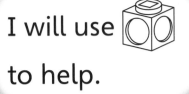

I will use to help.

$4 + 3 = 7$

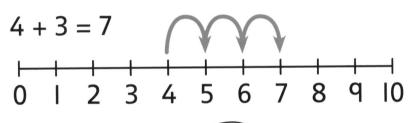

There are ☐ 🍩 in total.

I will put all the together.

b)

2 🍩 are eaten.

$7 - 2 = 5$

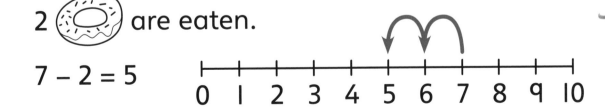

There are ☐ 🍩 left.

Think together

1 There are 4  in the sack.

How many are there altogether?

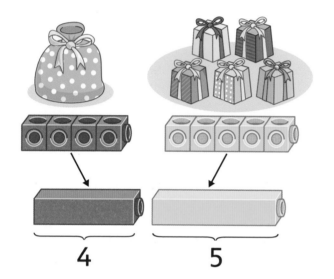

4   5

☐ + ☐ = ☐

There are ☐ altogether.

2 There are 8 in the bag.

5 are eaten.

How many are left?

8 ◯ ☐ = ☐

There are ☐ left.

3 How many  are there in total?

4   6   ☐ ◯ ☐ = ☐

There are ☐  in total.

I put the 🧊 together.

Count the 🧊 carefully.

159

→ Practice book 1A p114

End of unit check

Your teacher will ask you these questions.

1 Rav has 7 . He eats 2 .

How many are left?

A 9 **B** 7 **C** 2 **D** 5

2 Which number sentence is correct?

A $8 - 2 = 10$ **C** $6 - 4 = 2$

B $8 = 10 - 3$ **D** $2 = 10 - 9$

3 Which number sentence does not match the diagram?

A $5 - 3 = 8$ **C** $8 - 3 = 5$

B $8 = 5 + 3$ **D** $3 = 8 - 5$

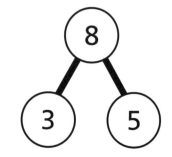

4 Which number sentence tells you how many more  than ◯ ?

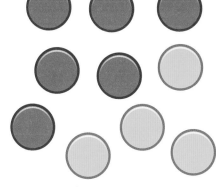

A $2 = 4 + 6$ **C** $6 = 4 - 2$

B $6 + 4 = 10$ **D** $6 - 4 = 2$

5 Which number could not go in the box?

$8 - 2 > 10 - \boxed{}$

A 10 **B** 5 **C** 6 **D** 3

Think!

Iris says she can see two facts.

$6 = 3 + 3$ $3 + 3 = 6$

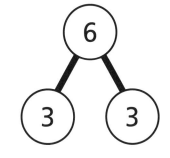

Marc says he can see three facts.

$6 - 3 = 3$ $3 - 6 = 3$ $3 = 6 - 3$

Explain the mistake that Marc has made.

These words might help you.

part   **whole**   **add**

subtract   **equals**   **take away**

161

→ Practice book 1A p117

Unit 5
2D and 3D shapes

In this unit we will …
- ⚡ Name 3D shapes
- ⚡ Name 2D shapes
- ⚡ Make patterns with shapes

Here are some shapes.
Can you name them?

We will need some shape words. Do you know some more shape words?

3D shape   **cube**   **cuboid**

sphere   **pyramid**   **cylinder**

cone   **2D shape**   **circle**

triangle   **rectangle**

faces   **pattern**

Which shape is the odd one out? Why?

Naming 3D shapes

Discover

These are all examples of **3D** shapes.

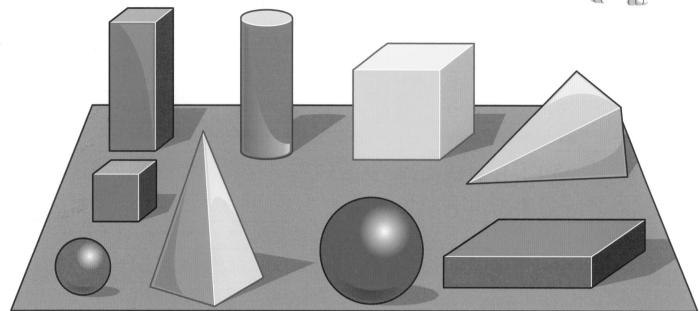

1 **a)** Put shapes with the same name together.

b) What is the shape without a pair?

Share

What is different about the **cube** and **cuboid**? Are they not the same?

The 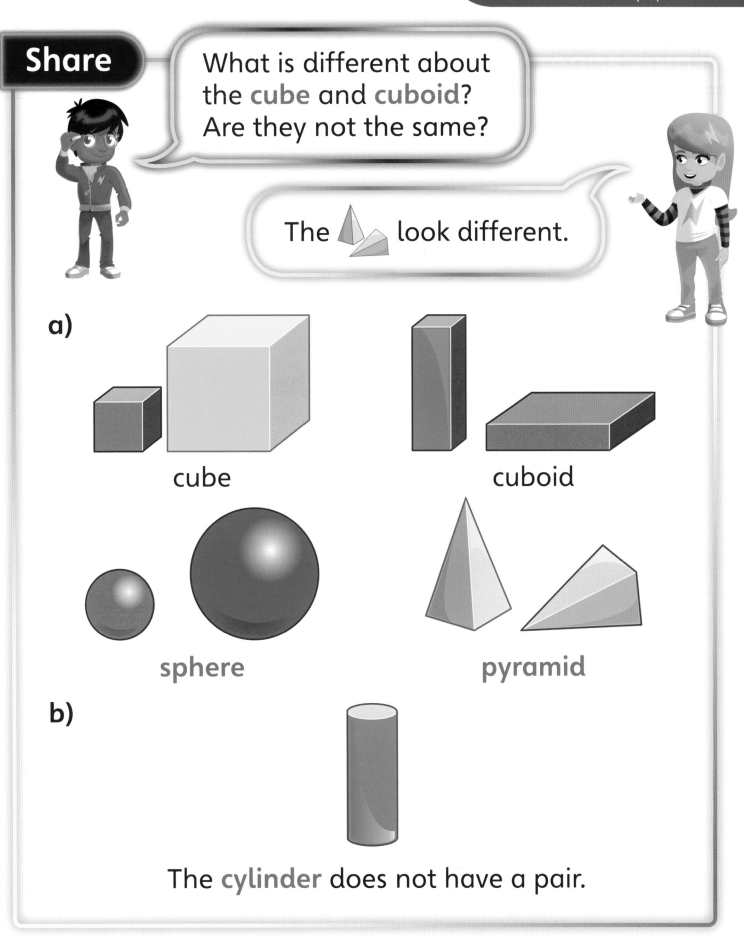 look different.

a)

cube

cuboid

sphere

pyramid

b)

The **cylinder** does not have a pair.

165

Think together

1 Find the cubes.

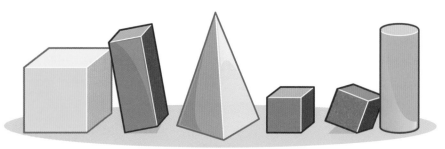

2 **a)** How many pyramids are there?

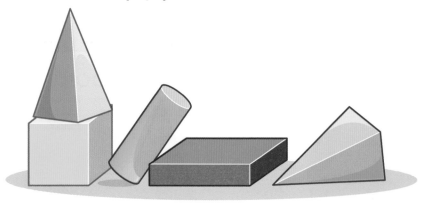

There are ☐ pyramids.

b) How many of the shapes are not spheres?

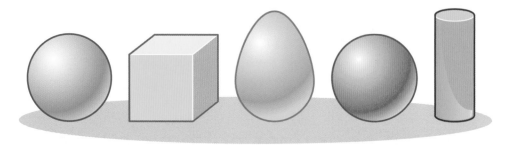

☐ of the shapes are not spheres.

3 Name these shapes.

CHALLENGE

 _____

 _____

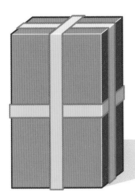 _____

 _____

The first one is just a football. Is that the name of the shape?

I cannot see a pyramid.

167

Naming 3D shapes ❷

Discover

Gita   Finn

1 **a)** Which rocket has broken?

b) Which of these shapes were not used?

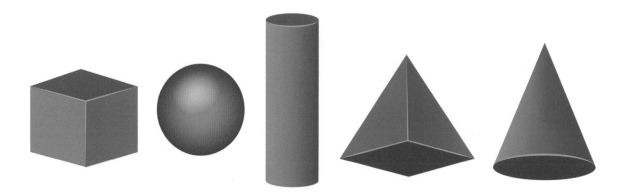

Share

I will draw the shapes.

Did they use the same shapes?

a)

 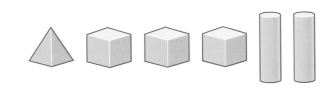

Finn used 1 pyramid, 3 cubes and 2 cylinders.

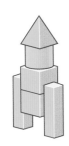 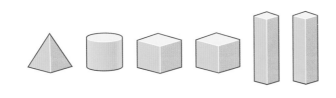

Gita used 1 pyramid, 1 cylinder, 2 cubes and 2 cuboids.

It must be Gita's rocket that is broken.

b)

 sphere    cone

The sphere and cone were not used.

169

Think together

1 Name the shapes.

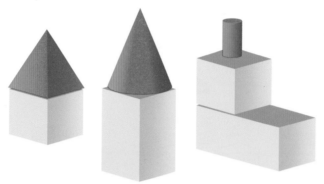

---

2 How many of each shape are there?

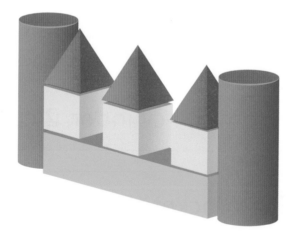

a) There are ☐ cuboids.

b) There are ☐ cylinders.

c) There are ☐ spheres.

d) There are ☐ pyramids.

3 How many cuboids are there?

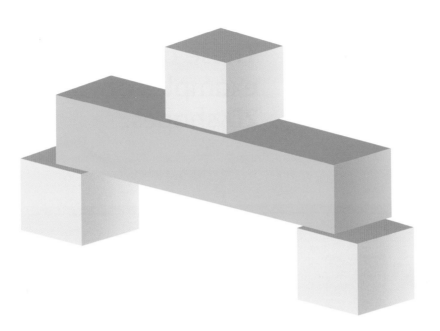

There are ⬜ cuboids.

Are cubes a kind of cuboid?

What is the same about all cubes?

171

→ Practice book 1A p122

Naming 2D shapes ❶

Discover

These are all examples of **2D** shapes.

❶ **a)** How many **circles** and **triangles** are there?

b) How many of the shapes are not triangles?

Share

a) circle

square

triangle

rectangle

other

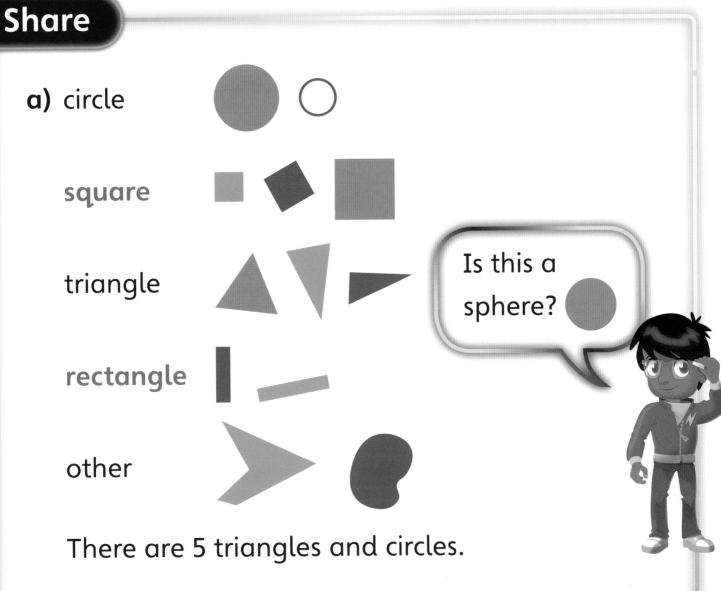

Is this a sphere?

There are 5 triangles and circles.

b)

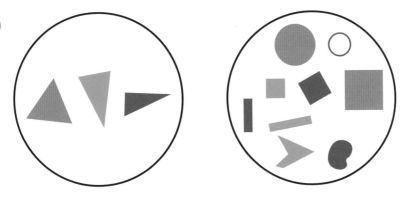

9 of the shapes are not triangles.

Think together

1 Find the squares and circles.

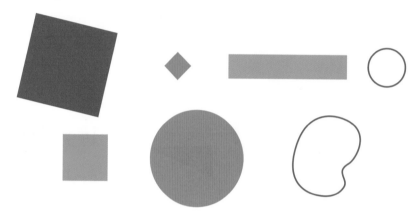

There are ☐ squares.

There are ☐ circles.

2 How many rectangles are there?

How many triangles are there?

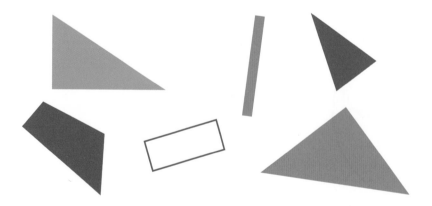

There are ☐ rectangles.

There are ☐ triangles.

CHALLENGE

3 Find the odd one out.

They all have
4 corners.

175

→ Practice book 1A p125

Naming 2D shapes ➋

1 **a)** Which 3D shapes did Irene use for the head and the body?

b) Which leg did Irene print first?

Share

A cube has square **faces**.

A cuboid can have square faces.

a)

Irene used the cube for the square head.

Irene used the cone and the cuboid for the body.

b)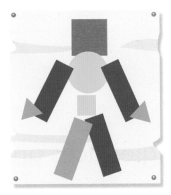

Irene printed the purple leg first because the green leg overlaps it.

177

Think together

1 What shapes can each cuboid print?

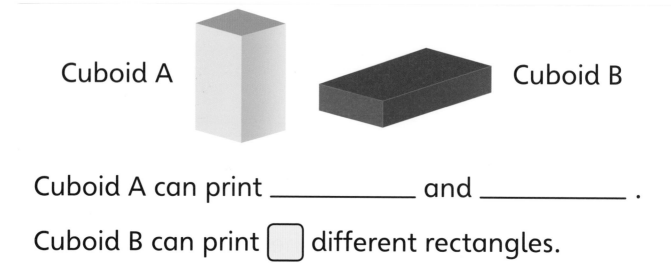

Cuboid A   Cuboid B

Cuboid A can print _____ and _____ .

Cuboid B can print ☐ different rectangles.

2 How many triangle faces are there?

How many square faces are there?

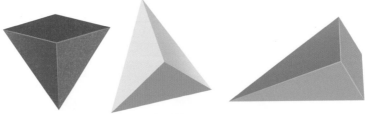

The ▼ has ☐ triangle faces and ☐ square face.

The ◢ has ☐ triangle faces and ☐ square faces.

The ◢ has ☐ triangle faces and ☐ square face.

178

3 Which shapes can print a circle?

CHALLENGE

A sphere looks like a circle.

I will try printing with a sphere.

→ Practice book 1A p128

Making patterns with shapes

Discover

Dear Sophie

You are invited to my party on Saturday 4th.

I hope you can come.

From Bilal

1 **a)** What shape is under the 🍵 ?

b) How many rectangles are on the invite?

Share

The **pattern** goes BIG, small, BIG, small…

Is it a yellow or a blue ?

a)

small **BIG** small **BIG** small **BIG** small **BIG**

There is 1 small circle under the .

b)

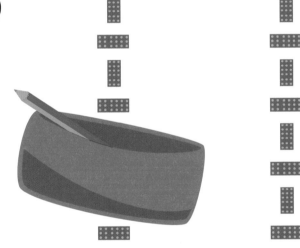

I can see 5 rectangles.

There are 3 covered.

$5 + 3 = 8$

There are 8 rectangles on the invite.

Think together

1 Which triangles are covered?

The pattern goes up, down, up, down…

It is _____ because

_____ .

2 Choose the shape to continue each pattern.

a)

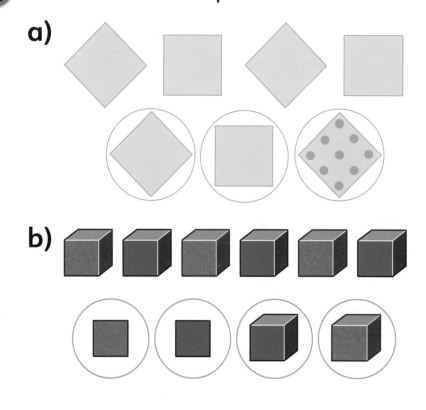

b)

3 What shape is hidden under the cap?

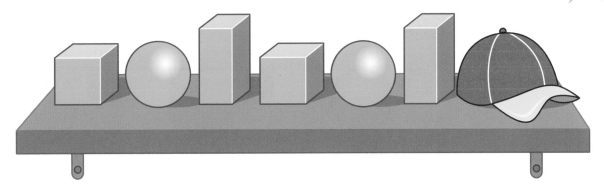

Can you explain the pattern?

This pattern has 3 **repeated** shapes.

This pattern uses 3D shapes.

→ **Practice book 1A p131**

End of unit check

Your teacher will ask you these questions.

1 Which is a sphere?

A  B  C  D

2 Which is not a cuboid?

A B 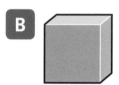 C  D

3 How many triangles?

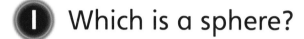

A 6 B 1 C 4 D 0

4 Which shapes are hidden?

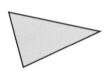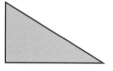

A square and rectangle C triangle and square

B square and circle D circle and rectangle

5 Which shape is not in this pattern?

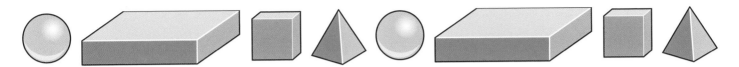

A pyramid

C triangle

B sphere

D cube

Think!

Where would you put this shape? Explain why.

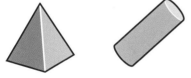

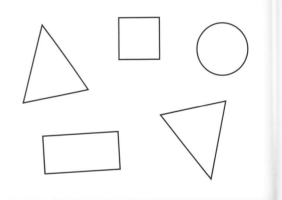

These words might help you.

dark   light   shape

2D   3D   group

185

→ Practice book 1A p134

Unit 6
Numbers to 20

In this unit we will ...
- ⚡ Count using tens and ones
- ⚡ Count one more and one less
- ⚡ Compare numbers of objects
- ⚡ Compare and order numbers

We will use tens to help count.
How many are there?

We will need some maths words. Which words do you already know?

One more

One less

Order

We need this too! Which numbers are missing?

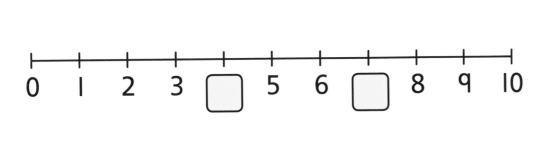

Counting and writing numbers to 20

Discover

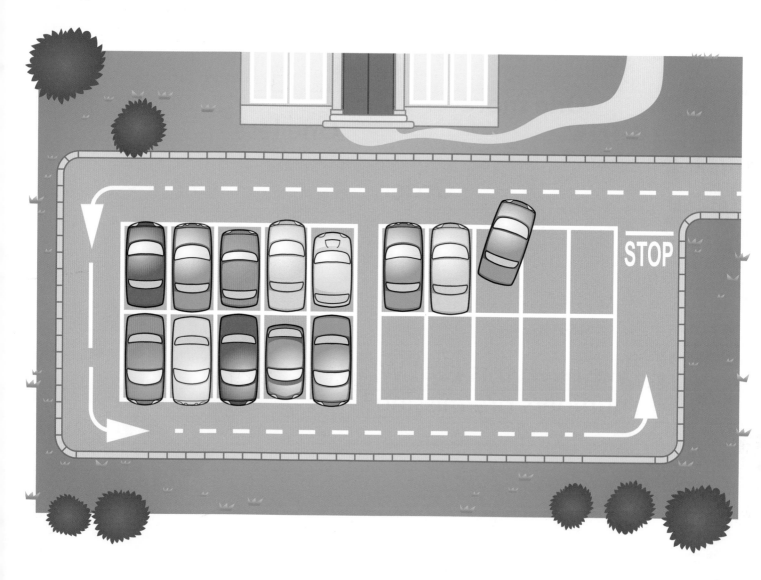

1 How many cars are there?

Can you count the cars in two ways?

Share

I counted the cars one by one.

Use ◯ on a ▭ to show the cars.

1 2 3 4 5   11 12 13

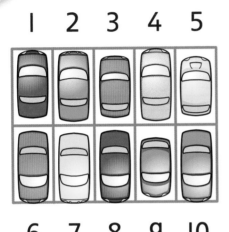

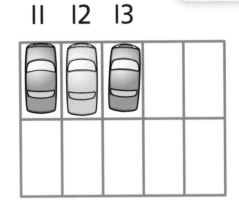

6 7 8 9 10

I saw 10 cars and then counted 3 more.

10   11 12 13

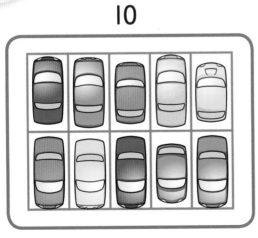

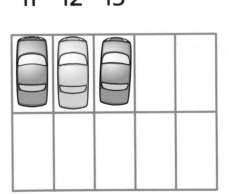

There are 13 cars.

Think together

1 How many cars are there now?

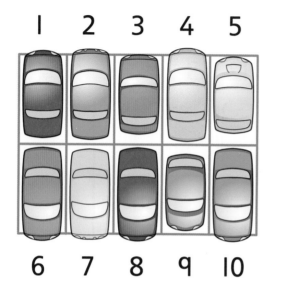

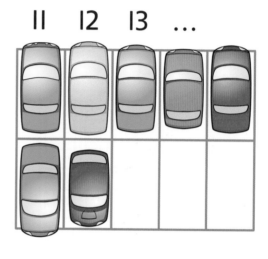

There are ☐ cars now.

2 The car park is full. How many cars are there now?

There are ☐ cars now.

3 The cars leave one by one.

Count backwards as they leave.

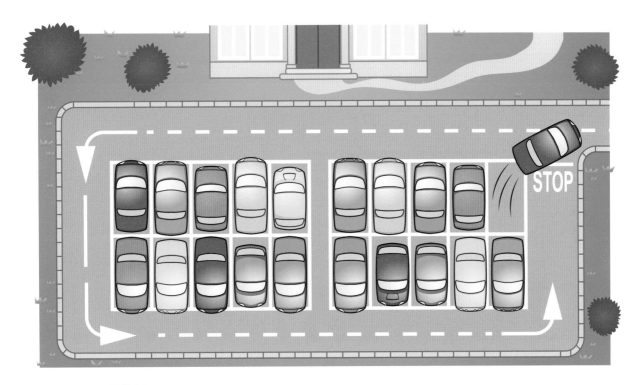

20, 19, 18, 17 …

Let's see if we can count quicker!

191

→ Practice book 1A p136

Tens and ones ①

Discover

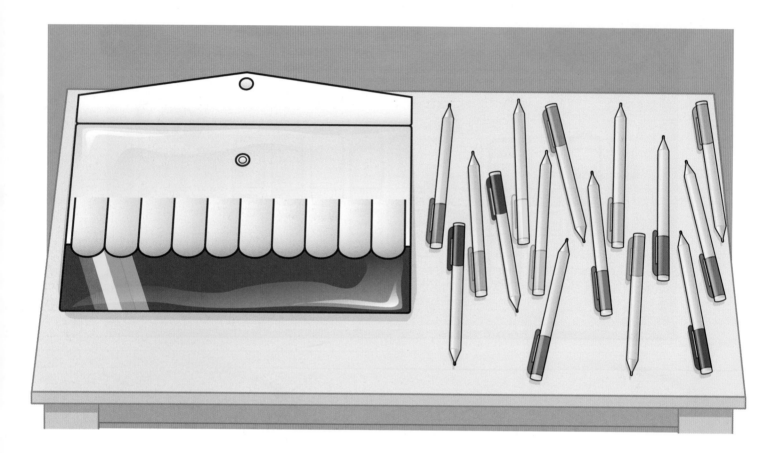

① **a)** How many ✏️ are there?

b) How many ✏️ fit in a pack?

Share

a)

I counted the 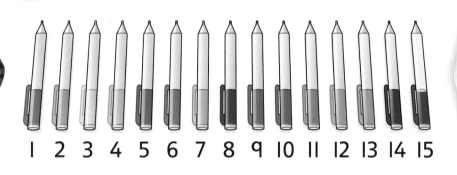 one by one.

Use ◯ on a ▭ to show the ✏.

1 2 3 4 5 6 7 8 9 10 11 12 13 14 15

There are 15 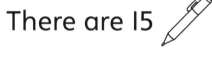 .

b)

I put some ✏ in the pack.
10 ✏ make one lot of ten.

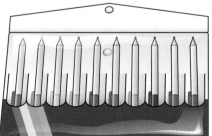

1 ten   5 ones

10  fit in a pack.

There is 1 **ten** and 5 **ones**.

There are 15 .

Think together

1 There is I pack of ten and 3 more. How many are there?

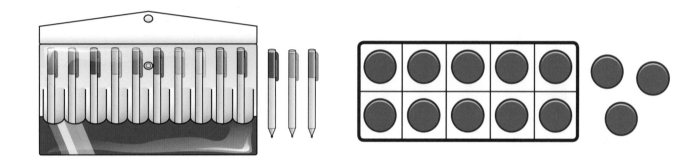

There are ▢ .

2 How many are there in 2 packs?

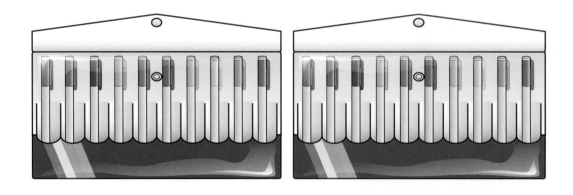

There are ▢ in 2 packs.

CHALLENGE

3 How many are there?

How many tens are there?

How many ones are there?

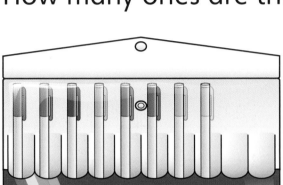 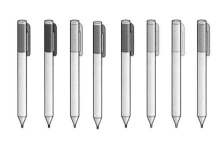

There are ▢ .

There is ▢ ten and ▢ ones.

There is one pack
and 8 more.
I think there are 18 .
Am I right?

Is the
pack full?

195

→ Practice book 1A p139

Tens and ones ②

Discover

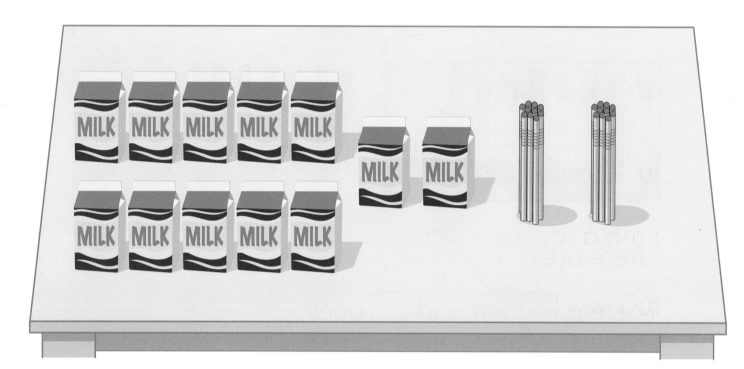

1 **a)** How many 🥛 are there?

b) How many 🥤 are there?

There are 10 🥤 in each 〰️.

196

Share

a)

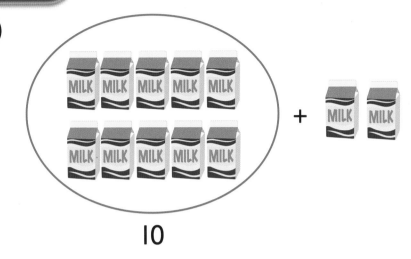

+

Use ◯ on a ⬚⬚⬚⬚⬚ to show the MILK.

10

10 MILK and 2 more MILK is 12.

1 ten and 2 ones = 12.

10 + 2 = 12

There are 12 MILK.

b)

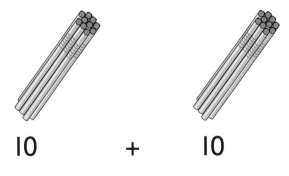

10   +   10

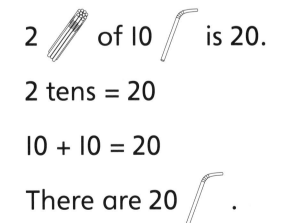

2 of 10 is 20.

2 tens = 20

10 + 10 = 20

There are 20.

Think together

1 How many  are there?

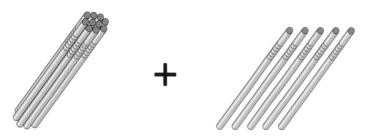

There is ☐ ten and ☐ ones.

☐ + ☐ = ☐

There are ☐  .

2 How many 🥛MILK are there?

There is ☐ ten and ☐ ones.

☐ + ☐ = ☐

There are ☐ 🥛MILK .

3 Is the number of children,  and the same?

Explain to your partner how you counted each group.

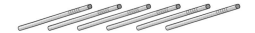

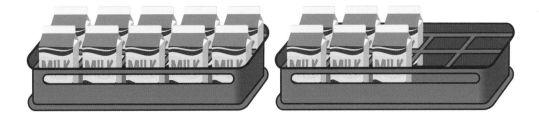

I can count each group in different ways.

199

→ Practice book 1A p142

Counting one more, one less

Discover

1 **a)** There are 12 children waiting in the line for lunch.

One more child joins the line.

How many children are there now?

b) One child gets lunch.

How many children are waiting now?

Share

I can use a to show how many children there are.

a)

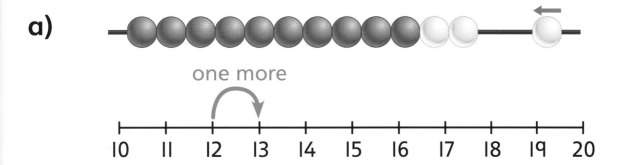

one more

There are 12 children waiting.

One more child joins the line.

One more than 12 is 13.

There are 13 children waiting now.

b)

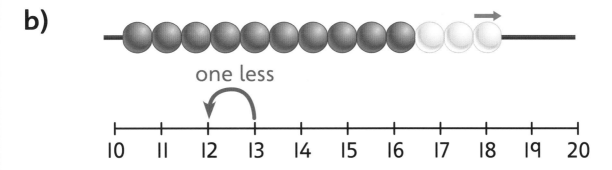

one less

One child gets lunch.

One less than 13 is 12.

There are 12 children waiting now.

Think together

1 Show me one more than 11.

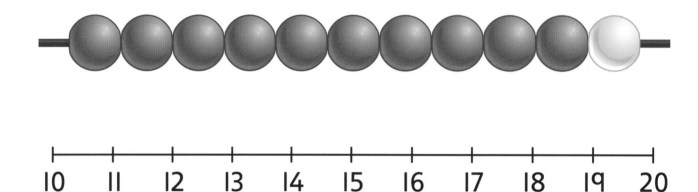

One more than 11 is ☐.

2 Show me one less than 10 + 6.

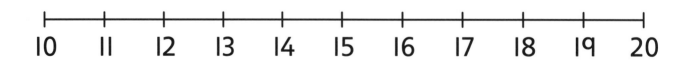

One less than 10 + 6 is ☐.

3 What is one more than 1 ten and 3 ones?

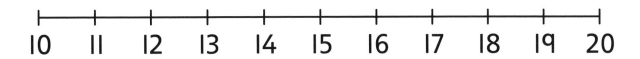

One more than 1 ten and 3 ones is ⬜ .

Do the ones change or do the tens change?

Does this happen with any number?
1 more than 14 =
1 more than 17 =
1 more than 19 =
1 less than 20 =

203

Comparing numbers of objects

Discover

1 How many  does Sam have?

How many does Tom have?

Who has **more** ?

Share

I can see Tom has more !

But Sam has that we cannot see. Let's line up the to see who has more.

Sam

Tom

Sam has 1 ten and 4 ones. He has 14 .

Tom has 1 ten and 1 one. He has 11 .

14 > 11

Sam has more .

Think together

1 Who has fewer 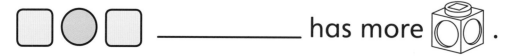 ?

Roz

Charlie

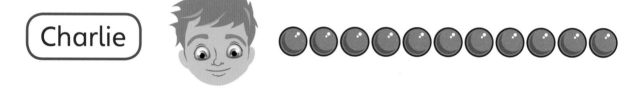 _____ has fewer .

2 Who has more ?

Meg

Abdi

 _____ has more .

3 Who has the **fewest** , Abby or Mia?

 Abby

 Mia

 _____ has the fewest .

 I think that the longer the line, the bigger the number.

 Is that always true?

207

→ **Practice book 1A p148**

Comparing numbers

Discover

Class I's favourite film

	Votes
Dino Adventure	1 2 3 4 5 6 7 8 9 10 11 12 13 14 15
Space Fun	1 2 3 4 5 6 7 8 9 10 11 12 13 14 15 16 17 18

1 Which film got the **most** votes?

Can you show the number of votes in two ways?

Share

I have shown the number of votes using 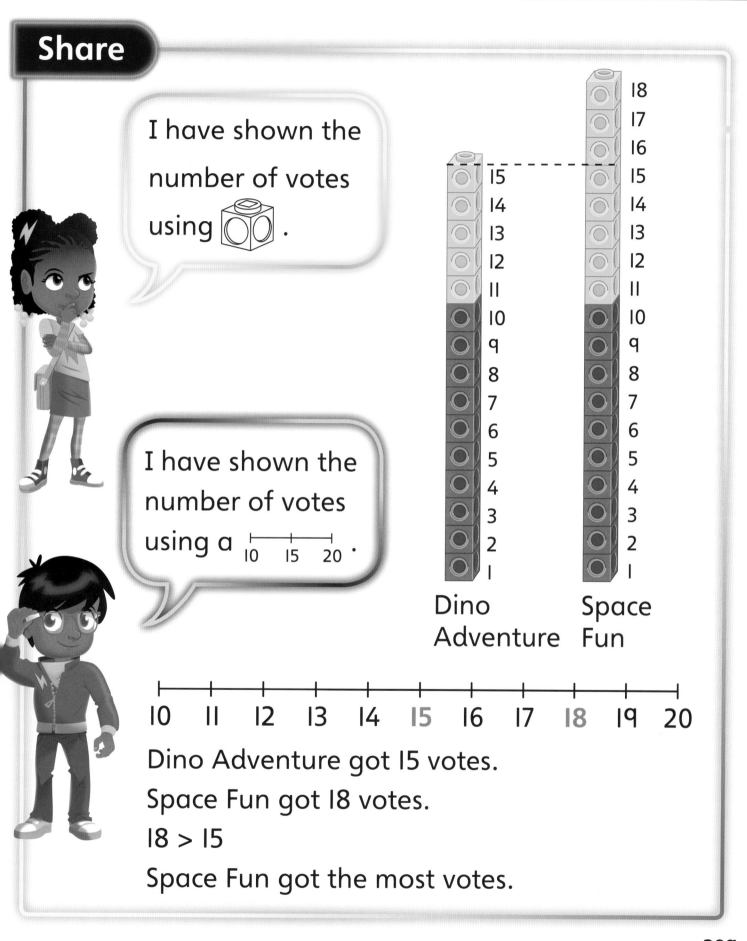.

I have shown the number of votes using a 10 15 20.

Dino Adventure

Space Fun

10 11 12 13 14 **15** 16 17 **18** 19 20

Dino Adventure got 15 votes.

Space Fun got 18 votes.

18 > 15

Space Fun got the most votes.

Think together

1 Which colour got the most votes?

 orange  12

 blue 9

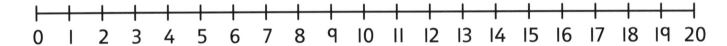

0 1 2 3 4 5 6 7 8 9 10 11 12 13 14 15 16 17 18 19 20

 > ☐

_____ got the most votes.

2 Which colour got the **least** votes?

green  15   pink  18

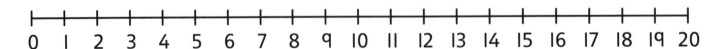

0 1 2 3 4 5 6 7 8 9 10 11 12 13 14 15 16 17 18 19 20

_____ got the least votes.

3 Which colour got the most votes?

purple  **13**   yellow **13**

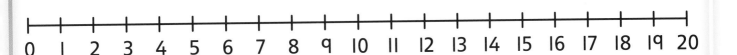

0 1 2 3 4 5 6 7 8 9 10 11 12 13 14 15 16 17 18 19 20

_____ got the most votes.

Can we use the < or > symbol?

211

→ Practice book 1A p151

Ordering objects and numbers

Discover

Anya   Billy   Dan

1 **a) Order** the number of sweets from least to most.

b) Who has the most sweets?

Share

a)

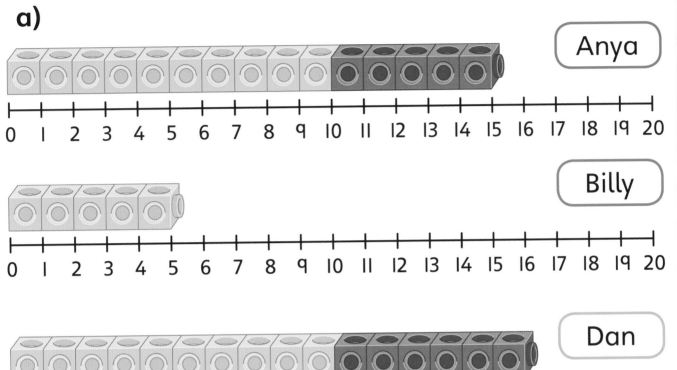

Anya

Billy

Dan

5 is **less than** 15.

15 is less than 16.

5 < 15 < 16

I don't think you have to count them all to put them in order. Can you see who has the least straight away?

b) 16 is **greater than** 5.

16 is greater than 15.

Dan has the most sweets.

Think together

1 Put the numbers 16, 19 and 12 in order.

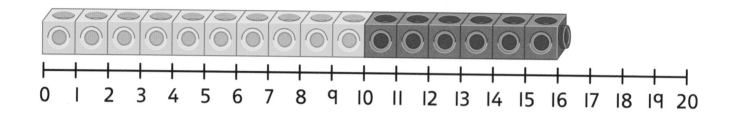

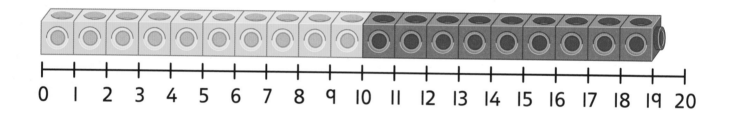

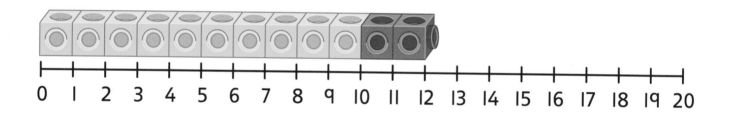

☐ is less than ☐

☐ is less than ☐

☐ < ☐ < ☐

2 Order the numbers, starting with the **smallest**.

14   16   13

$\boxed{}$ < $\boxed{}$ < $\boxed{}$

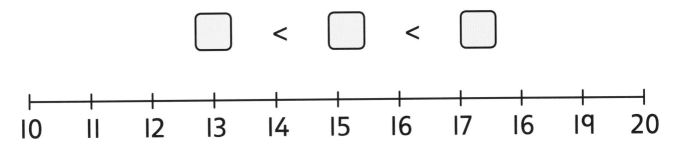

3 Which numbers could go in the boxes?

CHALLENGE

13 < $\boxed{}$ < 17   17 > $\boxed{}$ > 13

13 < 17 < $\boxed{}$

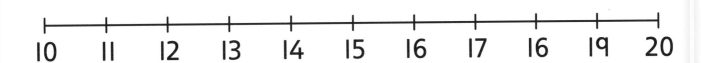

Is there more than one answer?

215

→ Practice book 1A p154

End of unit check

Your teacher will ask you these questions.

1 What number comes next?

sixteen, fifteen, fourteen, _____

A threeteen

C thirty

B thirteen

D three

2 Which answer does not match the ten frames?

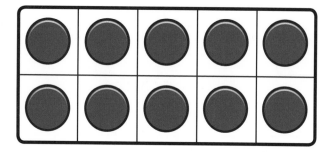 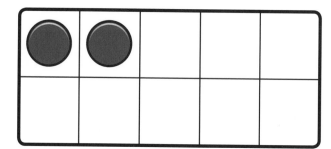

A twelve

C I ten and 2 ones

B 12

D I one and 2 ones

3 One more than ☐ is 10 + 4.

A 15

B 13

C 5

D 11

4 $10 + 9 < \boxed{}$

   A 19   **B** 18   **C** 10 + 8   **D** 20

5 Which number can complete the number sentence?

   $18 > \boxed{} > 15$

   A 19   **B** 15   **C** 17   **D** 14

Think!

Which is the odd one out?

Explain why.

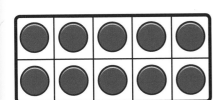 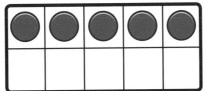

one more than 14

thirteen

10 + 5

These words might help you.

tens   ones

more than   less than

→ Practice book 1A p157

What do we know now?

Can you do all these things?

- ⚡ Work with numbers up to 10
- ⚡ Use a part-whole diagram
- ⚡ Add and subtract within 10
- ⚡ Recognise and name shapes
- ⚡ Work with numbers up to 20

Don't forget to keep practising!

Now you're ready for the next books!

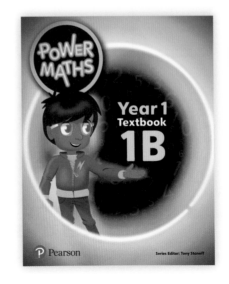

Power Maths Year 1 Textbook 1B

Pearson   Series Editor: Tony Staneff

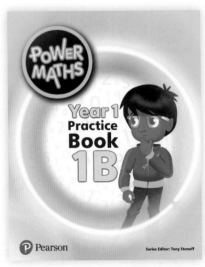

Power Maths Year 1 Practice Book 1B

Pearson   Series Editor: Tony Staneff